21 Traps

You Need to Avoid in Dating & Relationships.

It's time to take back your power!

What you will learn in this book:

The author of this book does not dispense medical advice or prescribe the use of any technique as a form of treatment for physical, emotional or medical problems without the advice of a qualified physician, either directly or indirectly. The intent of the author is only to offer information of a general nature to help you in your quest for emotional and spiritual well-being. In the event you use any of the information in this book, the author and the publisher assume no responsibility for your actions.

I wrote this book for you

I wrote this book because I respect you, a woman, more than you will ever know. Since 2008, I've been coaching women, and it hurts to see how my clients create self-fulfilling prophecies in their relationships. Every one of them deserves a good-looking guy who treats them well. Usually, these women get in trouble because they don't understand the way the mind of a man really works.

Some of the examples I provide in this book are very poignant. Some may offend you; others might even upset you. You may even think I'm childish or immature for my suggestions and advice. I can assure you, however, I'm not. I'm a man; I know how men think, and I want to uncover my gender's crazy reactions to what women do and don't do.

If you're willing to change some of your dating strategies and transform your thinking, you'll be surprised what's possible. The man you want will be kissing your feet in no time, or you'll be able to decide he's just not worth it because he simply cannot commit to you.

My goal is to spare you as much hurtful feelings as possible. Although I'm a man myself, I hate the way some men make women feel. These are the men you should avoid, and I'll discuss them as we discuss the various traps in dating. Once you're aware of the different relationship snares, you'll be able to avoid them altogether. You'll no longer set yourself up for bad relationships.

The red line in this book is that you shouldn't adapt. You shouldn't change who you are for any man; you shouldn't try to please. You should, instead, know what you're worth, know what you deserve, and be willing to walk away when the guy in your life doesn't measure up. Being willing to walk away will make you a lot more attractive to the man in your life, and that's only the tip of the iceberg.

Before we get started, ask yourself two simple questions:

1. On a scale from 1 to 10, what's the level of importance you gave yourself in your last dating relationships?
2. What's the level of importance you gave him?

Please, really take a minute to think about your answers before you continue reading.

The minute you make a man more important than yourself, your relationship is headed for trouble. Men have built-in radars for this. They all want a woman who has the confidence to know her worth. They want someone who knows her attention, her love, needs to be earned. Men want to earn a women's affection; they want to chase her, work hard to get her, and then, very importantly, work hard to keep her.

Will you allow yourself to be chased?

Women who go in the opposite direction often stay with men who are not ready to commit and hope it will change in the future. They try to adapt and please their man, doing whatever it takes to make him happy. That's a mistake. Your happiness is more important. You deserve it.

As you read through this book, you might think: "I'm not stupid! Some of what you write is too obvious. This is just advice for low-value or totally unattractive women." It will be very normal for you to think that, but it's dead wrong.

You should see the women I coach. They're successful, attractive, have their stuff together. Their love lives, however, often look like a jungle with a hidden minefield. Unknowingly, they step on these mines and wind up hurt, single, and thoroughly confused. It doesn't matter what you look like, how smart you are, or how successful you are. All women will make at least some of the mistakes this book discusses. Some might be stepping into these traps without even realizing it.

In the following pages, you'll learn all twenty-one traps and pitfalls of relationships that most women fall for. I'll show you how to avoid these snares and how to have a more fulfilling love life.

Read this book with an open mind. If you come across something you think is obvious, ask yourself:
1. I know this, but am I actually applying it?
2. Have I really never stepped into this trap?

Be honest with yourself. Your answers might surprise you.

Good luck!
Brian

Trap One: Giving Away Your Power

Sarah, one of my clients, met Mark at a company party. Mark seemed really interested in her since he was the one who walked up to her -- albeit a bit nervous -- introduced himself, and eventually asked for her phone number.

She was open to meeting new men but was tentative, proceeding with caution when a new man entered into her life. Since she had a past filled with bad relationships with cheaters and commit-phobic men, Sarah decided to take things slow. Although her professional life looked great, she couldn't help but wonder why all of her friends managed to be in seemingly happy relationships. As she saw a steady stream of happy pictures on social media, she started to feel unhappy about her own achievements in her love life. Shouldn't she be in a serious relationship by now? She was thirty-five, after all.

Mark was special. He couldn't be compared to the other men she had dated. One date was most often all it took for Sarah to feel disconnected from her date. The men she met all wanted sex, had no ambition or still lived with their mother; most were pretentious, narcissistic, and tried to buy her love with money. Mark, on the other hand, was really authentic, open, and honest.

His schedule, however, was pretty packed. Sarah felt as if she had to compete with his work, colleagues, friends, and so many other things since the beginning of their relationship. Even setting up that first date felt like booking an appointment with the president.

Whenever they were together, it was magical. Whenever they were apart, Sarah wondered when they would meet again. She tried to ask *him* out for a date as well, but he was always too busy to find an opening in his agenda. They met up at least once per week, but it always went the same way. Mark would call her up and ask: "Hey, can I come over tonight? We can have dinner first at [insert fancy restaurant] and then go over to your place."

These same-day dates became the norm. Whenever they made plans in advance, Mark often had to cancel them when something else came up. This continued for months before Sarah came to see me. She was living in a twilight zone and was slowly but surely losing herself.

Although Sarah is a very smart woman, it didn't surprise me that she had stepped into an important trap: she had given away her power. She was no longer in control. Instead, Mark led the relationship; he held all the cards. Sarah was simply at his whim, agreeing to go on a date whenever he called and never protesting when he had to cancel. He decided where the relationship was going and at what speed.

Reactive Mode

By slipping into reactive mode, Sarah gave away her power and let him take the lead 100% of the time. This is a trap commonly found with busy, successful, or A-type personality men.

Men love to chase after a woman and it's best to let him take those first steps. This doesn't mean you should go through the motions in a relationship. You will be dissatisfied and unhappy in the end if you let the man always lead, regardless of the circumstances. Feelings of helplessness -- the feeling that you cannot control the outcome no matter what you do -- are very harmful to your emotional well-being.

Take charge. Taking control isn't about acting needy or coming across as insecure, so here's what I asked Sarah to do. Whenever Mark called and asked her out on a same-day date, Sarah was supposed to decline by saying, "Sorry, tonight won't be a good time. I already have other plans." And then I asked her to be silent and wait.

This is crucial. If Sarah had elaborated or become uncomfortable during the moment of silence, it would have lowered her value. It was important for her not to come across as someone seeking his permission or someone who was feeling guilty. That would hand him the power.

This served another goal as well. By telling him that she had plans, Mark could now wonder, "What's she up to? What's more important than me? I'll need to up my game and give her more of my time and presence."

This strategy was not based on a hunch, I've been coaching women since 2008 and have seen this work countless times. Men always value what they have to work for.

Sarah had been consistently lowering her value by always adapting and being available whenever Mark called. She gave up her power. When Sarah said "no," Mark could react in multiple ways. He might have asked for an explanation or made a big deal about her continuing to say, "I'm busy" whenever he called for a last-minute date (thus presuming she would be free, or worse, would adapt her schedule to fit with his).

If Mark gave her any trouble, I asked Sarah to say, "You know, Mark, you must have me mistaken for a woman who doesn't have a life of her own, who's just waiting for you to call in order to see you. I'd love to see you, but I've got a full life too, so you'll need to give me a longer heads up. How about next Tuesday?"

I was happy that Sarah had contacted me before this relationship was going south, which they always do when a woman gives away her power. She was able to turn things around, avoid the other traps I'll talk about in this book, and is still in a happy relationship with Mark as of this writing. He's still very busy, but he never takes her for granted and continues to treat her with respect, gives her affection, and gladly includes her as a top priority in his full agenda.

Your love life is an important aspect of your life, and you should not give that power away. Ever. As you'll learn later in this book, it remains important to allow the man to chase you first. You'll often hear me say men are supposed to do the chasing, and that remains crucial. Allowing him to chase you doesn't mean you need to hand over the steering wheel. When you don't give away your power, you'll simultaneously allow and force him to chase you more.

Never adapt to a man who doesn't adapt to you. Never change plans for a man who doesn't change his plans for you.

Please know that many smart women fall into this trap because they are blinded by love. They prefer to get a very small piece of him instead of getting nothing at all. That seems logical, but any woman who's prepared to sit by the sidelines will be perceived as low value, especially by high-value men like Mark.

Trap Two: Failing an Important Test

Have you ever seen or heard about the marshmallow test? Psychologist Walter Mischel from Stanford University conducted the marshmallow experiment in the late 1960s.

The setup of the experiment was simple. A child between the ages of 7 and 9 was sitting at a table in a room with no distractions at all. Someone would put a marshmallow (or a cookie) on the table in front of him or her. The child is then told if the cookie remains uneaten while the researcher leaves the room for about 15 minutes, the child will get two marshmallows or cookies when the researcher returns.

As the researcher (often a woman) left, the scene that unfolded was often funny. Some children would go through great lengths to prevent themselves from eating the marshmallow. Some covered their eyes; others hid the marshmallow, and others played with it to keep busy. Some succumbed after a couple of minutes and ate the marshmallows; while some, of course, ate it as soon as the researcher had left.

This was an important test about delayed gratification and emotional intelligence. Some children clearly went for instant gratification while others tried to use their limited amounts of self-control to get more gratification later when the amount of cookies would be doubled.

These children have then been followed throughout their lives, and it quickly became clear that those who could muster up the courage and emotional intelligence to wait for the researcher to return got further ahead in life. This was true in all areas of their lives: financially, romantically, professionally, etc.

Some people were born with a strong self-control muscle; others had to train themselves and consciously weigh the future consequences of every decision in order to pick the best one. Self-control, as you will see throughout this book, will be one of your assets with the biggest impact on the quality of your love life and romantic relationships.

It's simple. Going for instant gratification rarely provides great long-term results. That's pretty obvious when it comes to deciding whether you'll eat fast food versus a wholesome fresh meal. It's even more logical when we think about the financial decisions we make in life. But we rarely think about our love life when it comes to instant gratification. Most people believe their love life is the one area of life where they need to just be themselves, where they can indulge themselves.

This advice is passed on at a young age; "Just be yourself" is a phrase many mothers and fathers say to their children when they are facing the challenges of love and first relationships.

Contrary to popular belief, this is not the best advice we can get in relationships. Hardly any part of our lives can give us more emotions -- both good and bad -- than our love lives.

Our ability to not immediately act upon those emotions will be crucial if we want to have a healthy relationship. When we act upon feelings of anger, jealousy, or neediness, we become weaker in the relationship.

When you go for instant gratification in a relationship and just follow your heart and emotions, it will feel like you have control in the short term. In the long term, however, you will be destroying the very relationship you try to protect. Think of the woman who feels jealous when she sees another woman flirt with her boyfriend and acts upon that feeling by getting mad. Had she waited a couple of minutes longer, her boyfriend would have politely turned down the other woman.

Not using self-control in a romantic relationship will create a whole range of issues and problems. Firstly, you might create negative moments, fights, jealous outbursts and more where it was not needed. Secondly, you are essentially giving away your power to the other person. When you always act upon your emotions, you are showing other people how to manipulate you. The tactic is simple; they evoke an emotion and you will act upon it. If they want you to become more interested in them, they make you jealous. If they want to string you along and calm you down, they simply have to show some love and give some attention or promise you that he will change. Handing away this type of control over you can be very dangerous when you meet a manipulative man.

Here's how this will work. When a man finds out how to change your emotions, he has gained control over you. Emotions are a woman's Achilles heel, so to speak. It's how manipulative men control the actions of their partner.

Here are some examples:

1. Lying to you
2. Switching from hot to cold to play with your heart
3. Playing hard to get
4. Giving you a false sense of security
5. Trying to dictate your time and actions

6. Promising that he will change when he darn well knows he has no intention to

Most bad men will push you into a reactive state. So they'll do something, say something, or avoid doing something to get a specific reaction from you.

Think about this. Every time a man made you do something you later regretted, more often than not it's because you reacted to a manipulative strategy he just deployed. You followed your emotions instead of using your head.

Enter emotional intelligence. Emotional intelligence, simply put, is the power to look beyond your emotions and see the long-term consequences of the action you want to take and decide if that's where you really want to be heading. Being emotionally intelligent means not following your feelings or instincts and taking the time to get some altitude, have an honest look at what's happening, and then deciding what action you want to take. It's never about simply reacting or immediately trusting and following your gut or your heart.

You might already be very good at this. If this is nevertheless still challenging to you and your emotions rule your actions more than you would like, then it's time to practice your self-control muscles. At first, you will not be able to control your emotions. They are instinct-like reactions programmed to pop up. That's fine, because we can still decide how we react to them.

I personally have had to learn how to use self-control while I drive when I was still a young 24-year-old. Being a pretty laid-back guy outside of my car, I became a monster, a true narcissist, when I was driving. I thought I owned the road and whenever someone else did something to deliberately block me, slow me down, or even just annoy me by driving too close behind me on the freeway, my heart would start to pound faster. My face would turn red, and I would go into full-attack mode. It must have been a silly sight.

It took me a while before it dawned on me what a fool I was making of myself. And not just that, but I was giving those other people too much power over my emotions. I gave them permission to raise my heart rate, to drive like a fool, and get angry. I gave them control over me, and that's the last thing these people deserved.

The same scenario happens in relationships. During the many years I've been coaching women, I've had super intelligent women as clients; successful women who would still hand away their power to men who where just playing games with them. Men who didn't deserve to get that power. These men pulled their strings by being disrespectful and using manipulative techniques to string those women along.

This happens rather quickly. First you'll feel an emotion, a gut-level reaction, an instinctive urge. This is the part we cannot really control. This is where the child smells and sees the marshmallow and thinks, "Gosh, that little thingy will taste SOOOO good when I eat it!" This is where a guy does anything or fails to do something that, as a result, gives you a negative or a positive emotion. And that's where we'll need to make a split-second decision and decide to simulate what action from our part will have the best long-term consequences.

Take a couple of seconds to step back and analyze what's really best for you, regardless of what your urge, your emotions, or your instincts are telling you. You can and will dramatically change your future and the quality of your finances, relationships, career, and more.

Both negative and positive emotions need your attention. Some needy women fall into the positive emotion trap. They meet a guy they like, he asks them out, and when they get engulfed by positive emotions of love, happiness, and bliss they move ahead full force, turn around the roles, and start chasing the guy with all they have...only to come across as super needy.

Whenever you feel a strong urge or emotion in a relationship, it's useful to take a step back, look at what's happening, and then decide what's best for you in the long term.

It turns out there are ways to step on the brake and go in another direction once we have felt an initial emotion. This is where your self-control enters the game. Getting better at applying a healthy dose of self-control has given both my clients and myself a lot of success in every area of our lives. You will, however, need to actually train it, like a muscle.

Self-control will greatly increase your powers over men. In any relationship, he or she who controls their emotions the best has the power and the lead.

Self-control is hard. Resisting an urge uses a lot of brainpower of which we only have a limited supply every day. And yet self-control is the secret of many who became successful in life. Self-control is about inhibition; it's stopping a thought or an emotional response and choosing a different path.

Here's a great visual example. It's the "Stroop" test as scientists call it. Please read the color of the text below out loud. Don't read the actual word, but say the color of the text.

Black

Gray

Gray

Black

Did you get in trouble?

Most people do, as of the third word. It says, "gray," but the font color is black. Your mind has the urge, the tendency, to simply read the word instead of saying the color. That's the easiest path, the path of least resistance.

For you to say "black" takes extra energy, since the color was black and not gray. It's as if you're mentally driving in a certain direction and then need to decide to hit the brakes, turn around, and go in a different direction. This is exactly what happens when you feel an emotion (jealousy, neediness, anxiety), an urge, and decide to take a different path. It's not easy, but that's OK.

I won't go into the technical details, but our ability to inhibit a thought, an emotion, and so on is found in the ventrolateral prefrontal cortex of the brain. The prefrontal cortex in the front of the brain uses a lot of energy. Practicing self-control and managing your emotions are hard tasks. It uses up energy, and we only have a set amount of energy we can use every day.

This can be pretty challenging when you're in a relationship with a man who makes you insecure, causes you to worry, and gives you a variety of emotions, both good and bad.

The trick to do this successfully is in the timing. The farther you went down a specific path, the harder it will get to change course. You'll need to act fast when the unwanted emotion arises. Dr. Jeffrey M. Schwartz studied this and calls it the "free won't." Instead of our free will, he says, we have a free won't, the option to choose not to follow the path, the emotion, the thought.

Whenever you feel a negative emotion like sadness, anger, anxiety, and so on, don't follow the urge or your instincts. Don't act on it yet. Take a step back, analyze what's going on, and decide how you should act to get the best long-term results. Simply saying, "No, I'm not going to get carried away by this" does wonders.

This will help with unwanted emotions in relationships, and it will reinforce you with unwanted emotions and distractions in every part of your life. Please try to apply it and test it out for yourself. You'll be surprised of the possibilities.

Resist the urgency you'll feel. Continue to focus on the long-term benefits and decide to no longer go for the quick fix. You might have tried going for the instant gratification before, and it probably didn't get you what you wanted, needed, or deserved. It's not worth it. Getting two marshmallows is always better than one; it's worth using up some of our self-control energy to get more of what we want later.

Trap Three: Beauty Isn't Everything

In the movie *Alfie*, Jude Law says, "For every beautiful woman out there, there's a man who's tired of *bleeping* her." That struck a chord with me. The first time I heard it I thought, "How rude and disrespectful to women!"

But as I dug a little bit deeper, I started to see more and more proof of his statement. We get used to anything and everything that surrounds us, everything that's easy to get, that's omnipresent. When you live in the mountains and love the sea, a beach visit makes you feel all happy and tingly inside. Should you then move to the beach and wake up with a beach view every single morning, that breathtaking view will no longer take your breath away. You won't dislike it, but it will feel normal and no longer special.

Are there aspects of your life that were once really special but now you consider normal? They no longer make your heart pound a little faster when you see it or experience it? These can be material items like a new phone or a sexy dress or it can be experiences like eating out in a restaurant or going to a specific holiday location or hotel. If you keep frequenting the same holiday location, you'll probably still like it, but it won't make you vibrate with happiness like it did the first time.

Alfie exaggerated a bit in his quote. I'm not sure we get tired of beauty or anything we once found valuable, but it surely won't be enough to make us keep us coming back for more, especially not when other "new" experiences keep knocking on our door.

I see women make a huge mistake when it comes to beauty. Gorgeous women believe their beauty is their biggest strength when it comes to men, dating, and relationships. They believe they have what men want the most. Not so beautiful women think they're doomed. They don't believe they'll get a good-looking and successful man because he can get better. Both types of women couldn't be more wrong. They base their theory on the wrong premise.

Before I dig into what smart men, real catches, think about beauty, let's look at an interesting Internet phenomenon concerning this subject. A beautiful woman many years ago posted this post on Craigslist, a classified ads site:

What am I doing wrong?

Okay, I'm tired of beating around the bush. I'm a beautiful (spectacularly beautiful) 25-year-old girl. I'm articulate and classy. I'm not from New York. I'm looking to get married to a guy who makes at least half a million a year. I know how that sounds but keep in mind that a million a year is middle class in New York City, so I don't think I'm overreaching at all.

Are there any guys who make 500K or more on this board? Any wives? Could you send me some tips? I dated a businessman who makes around 200 – 250. But that's where I seem to hit a roadblock. 250,000 won't get me to central park west. I know a woman in my yoga class was married to an investment banker and lives in Tribeca, and she's not as pretty as I am, nor is she a great genius. So what is she doing right? How do I get to her level?

Here are my questions specifically:

–Where do you single rich men hang out? Give me specific bars, restaurants, gyms.

–What are you looking for in a mate? Be honest guys, you won't hurt my feelings.

–Is there an age range I should be targeting (I'm 25)?

–Why are some of the women living lavish lifestyles on the upper east side so plain? I've seen really 'plain Jane' boring types who have nothing to offer married to incredibly wealthy guys. I've seen drop dead gorgeous girls in singles bars in the east village. What's the story there?

– Jobs I should look out for? Everyone knows – lawyer, investment banker, doctor. How much do those guys really make? And where do they hang out? Where do the hedge-fund guys hang out?

–How you decide marriage vs. just a girlfriend? I am looking for MARRIAGE ONLY.

Please hold your insults – I'm putting myself out there in an honest way. Most beautiful women are superficial at least I'm being up front about it. I wouldn't be searching for these kinds of guys if I wasn't able to match them in looks, culture, sophistication, and keeping a nice home and hearth.

As you know by now, it's never my goal to insult you. I know you would never think of posting something this silly! Yet I've met my fair share of super pretty women who have this exact mindset. And it's just wrong, really wrong.

A rich banker gave her a rather poignant response:

Dear Pers-431649184:

I read your posting with great interest and have thought meaningfully about your dilemma. I offer the following analysis of your predicament.

Firstly, I'm not wasting your time. I qualify as a guy who fits your bill; that is, I make more than $500K per year. That said, here's how I see it. Your offer, from the prospective of a guy like me, is plain and simple a crappy business deal. Here's why. Cutting through all the BS, what you suggest is a simple trade: you bring your looks to the party, and I bring my money.

Fine, simple. But here's the rub, your looks will fade and my money will likely continue into perpetuity...in fact, it is very likely that my income will increase, but it is an absolute certainty that you won't be getting any more beautiful!

So, in economic terms, you are a depreciating asset, and I am an earning asset. Not only are you a depreciating asset, your depreciation accelerates! Let me explain. You're 25 now and will likely stay pretty hot for the next 5 years, but less so each year. Then the fade begins in earnest. By 35, stick a fork in you!

So in Wall Street terms, we would call you a trading position, not a buy and hold...hence the rub...marriage. It doesn't make good business sense to "buy you" (which is what you're asking) so I'd rather lease. In case you think I'm being cruel, I would say the following. If my money were to go away, so would you, so when your beauty fades I need an out. It's as simple as that. So a deal that makes sense is dating, not marriage.

Separately, I was taught early in my career about efficient markets. So, I wonder why a girl as "articulate, classy, and *spectacularly beautiful" as you has been unable to find your sugar daddy. I find it hard to believe that if you are as gorgeous as you say you are that the $500K hasn't found you, if not only for a tryout.*

By the way, you could always find a way to make your own money and then we wouldn't need to have this difficult conversation. With all that said, I must say you're going about it the right way. Classic "pump and dump."

I hope this is helpful, and if you want to enter into some sort of lease, let me know.

When I read this the first time, I couldn't stop laughing. Both people had clearly never experienced real love or any form of meaningful relationship. Love is not a transaction. His response was, however, spot on.

Beauty is a depreciating asset. Women who put all their eggs in that basket are playing a game they can only lose.

I know you're smarter than that, and I'm in no way implying you're playing that game, but I need to restate it: beauty is overrated. Beauty and looks matter, but only for the so-called physical attraction test.

The Physical Attraction Test

In the hierarchy of needs and importance, looks matter more to men than they do to most women. Still, their value is overrated.

The physical attraction test occurs the first moment a guy looks at you and scans your body and face. This only takes him a short while to decide if you're a clear pass (or not).

Women do this as well, of course. But men take it one step further.

A man cannot have sex with a woman and cannot feel attracted to a women when she doesn't pass the physical attraction test. No Viagra in the world can help him when he doesn't find her attractive. He can be friends but nothing more.

When asked, most women will claim looks are important to them as well. Women can, however, still develop feelings for a guy they already know, who didn't pass the attraction test at first. I've met many women who only fell for a man after having known him for quite a while. Some even found that same guy unattractive at first, so he clearly did not pass the physical attraction test at that time.

Men cannot ignore the physical attraction test. They can and will only develop feelings for a woman who passes his physical attraction test. This is, in most cases, nothing you should ever worry about as a woman. When a guy flirts with you, dates you, kisses you, sleeps with you, and so on, you have clearly passed his physical attraction test. He would otherwise not spend that kind of time with you.

Your looks get your foot in the door, so to speak. That's all. Your personality, the way you feel about yourself, the way you make him feel, and so on will define whether he will stay and commit or not.

A man will initially be attracted to your looks, but it's your personality that can make him addicted to you. It's who you are on the inside that counts in the long term.

I've seen many examples of men who stayed madly in love with their woman, even though her looks were fading with age. No surgery was necessary since that man had fallen in love with her soul. The good news is this doesn't take years; it only takes a couple of months.

Sadly, many women often overlook this fact. They focus way too much on their physical appearance. If you want a guy to stick around, you'll need much more than looks. He needs to love your personality and your soul -- who you truly are on the inside. This might sound difficult; how on earth do you make him fall in love with your soul?

I'll give you the answers throughout this book. Stepping into any of the traps to avoid would prevent him from seeing your actual soul, let alone fall in love with it. When a woman plays games, plays hard to get, is afraid to show her true self to him he cannot look pass her looks.

In my private coaching practice, I've met a lot of women who lost their guy to a "young and beautiful woman." These women often complained about men being superficial, since they were just traded in for a prettier and often younger version. And sure, that's exactly what it looks like on the surface. The reality, however, is often different.

When I then start to coach these women and dig a little deeper, I often uncover what's really going on. Jessica was a great example of this.

Jessica, 43, woke up one morning only to find her estranged husband wanting to talk. He wanted to start the divorce procedure since things were not working out between them. John, her husband, moved in with his younger and prettier girlfriend less than two months later.

When she came to see me, she quickly exclaimed, "He traded me in for a younger and prettier version." Although that does indeed seem to be the case, there was more going on.

It turned out Jessica had transformed herself from the high-value woman she once was into a low-value slave who did everything she could to please John, so he wouldn't run away with another woman. She had created a self-fulfilling prophecy. When I asked her why she had pushed her own life and needs aside to please John, she told me, "Honestly, I think I did it because I was getting older, didn't like what I was seeing in the mirror, and wanted to make up for it by adapting to John's wishes, both real and implied."

That was a big mistake. As I dug deeper and deeper into what had happened the last couple of years, the truth started to unravel. Jessica, once a woman full of self esteem with hobbies, friends, a great career, a passion for long walks in nature with her dog and taking care of her body by working out and eating well had made a U-turn to morph herself into a much less attractive version of herself. She slowly started to make everything in her life about him. She had given up on her hobbies, stopped taking care of her body and mind, tried to please John by doing all of his laundry, cooking for him, taking care of him while she had her own career to look at for as well. This U-turn was initiated by the fear of losing him. And that's exactly what happened because of the changes she had made.

She failed to see that she had been losing her own self-respect. And the old adage always rings true: other people cannot respect you more than you respect yourself.

Love conquers a lot, but it cannot conquer this. A man who's madly in love with a woman will start to lose respect, attraction, and feelings for his girlfriend or wife when she doesn't love herself. This luckily is a slow process, but it always happens. I've seen it in action countless times.

Jessica thought John's leaving was linked to her decline in looks that came with age, whereas it was the changes in her personality that made him leave. I've seen Jessica and can confirm she was still a very good-looking woman. She had created the problem entirely in her own mind, because she followed her negative thoughts and gave them way too much importance.

She was focusing too much on her looks. Since she was an attractive woman when they met, she mistakenly believed this was one of the primary factors that made John stick around.

It's possible that you're thinking, "Look at the facts. He did leave her for a prettier woman, didn't he?" Yes, he did. But as I talked to Jessica, I saw there were clues in the relationship that were a clear proof of his declining interest in her. Those moments always happened when Jessica changed.

One weekend, while John was making plans with his male friends to hang out, Jessica had complained that he was leaving her alone. "What am I supposed to do when you are gone?" she said. "I want to have fun too. Please stay here." This was not only needy behavior, but John clearly responded, "Baby, you're right. I don't understand why you gave up on your piano lessons and most of your other hobbies. You used to have so many activities that made you happy, whereas now it seems like you only have me to make you happy." That was a spot-on analysis from John. This was not the only red flag, of course, but most of them pointed in this direction. John was starting to feel the pressure and even though they had been in a long-term relationship, she was strangling him slowly but surely and thus raising his fear to stay committed...to her.

Jessica had become needy; she had made John her one and only priority, her only source of happiness. And that's always a big mistake. This started to suffocate John; it took the fun out of the relationship, made him feel guilty when he wanted to spend time with his friends, and so on. That change in her personality was what pushed him away, not her decline in looks.

If men only care about looks, why then do we see so many normal-looking women with great and good-looking guys who could get better if we solely based us on the looks department? Why do we see happy older couples where the guy didn't trade in his wife for a younger model? I know 70-year-old couples who still flirt like teenagers.

It's because those women have magnetic personalities, because they know how to keep him walking on his toes and how to make him put in a continuous effort not to lose her! They are the high-value women who will never make their lives revolve solely around their man. They know they have more to offer than just their looks.

So in a way, this is the curse of the beautiful woman. As soon as her beauty starts to fade, she starts to lose her self-esteem and her personality. She thinks she's losing her value and all that she has to offer.

Things changed for Jessica the minute she started to worry about losing John. That's when the switch happened and when she started to adapt. Until that point, John had been doing his best not to lose her. And that's the position you should always put your guy in. At all times. Your guy should always feel lucky to be with you and at least fear the possibility that you might leave *him* some day. I'll teach you how to get into that position throughout this book.

Trap Four: Going Against the Grain

The fact that women have started to receive equality after the 50s has been truly important. It still bothers me that some men think women are less than men. They have no idea. Nevertheless, with that gained freedom and confidence come some dark shadows that make it harder for Cupid to find his way and aim straight.

Some women have taken over the role of the man in the game of courtship. They initiate the flirting, ask for the phone number, ask a guy out on a date, and take the lead. Although taking the lead works great in business and just about anywhere else, it's a trap in the romantic world. A woman should never give away her power and that's exactly what she does when she takes over the 'chasing'. She should let the man do the chasing, at all times.

There are two -- mostly overlooked -- reasons why it is absolutely crucial that the man takes the first step. The first reason is linked to our nature. Men do the picking; women do the choosing. This is how it has always worked for our species, and we shouldn't go against the grain. It's a man's job to initiate the courtship, to take the risk of rejection so the woman can then decide whether she wants to accept him or not. More on that part later.

The second reason is important for your sense of security and mental peace. The best way to gage the interest level a man has in you is to verify the amount of effort he makes in order to seduce you and/or keep you. You cannot verify this effort if you, the woman, are the one who's taking the lead and putting in all the hard work. **The general rule is: a man who likes you will help you.**

If you need to pull hard to reel him in, if you feel forced to do the chasing, something is wrong. You're going against the grain. Relationships are hard enough as it is, and if you already have to put in a lot of effort before the dating process or relationship has even started, then you're heading for a rocky future. You're strapping yourself in for an emotional rollercoaster ride since you'll be dealing with a guy whose interest level is simply not high enough toward you.

Men need a challenge; men need to hunt. Men and women are not alike. They should be equal in all aspects of life, but they should never be considered alike, because they aren't. Not on the outside, not on the inside. There is a huge list of biological and mental differences between men, some very significant.

So I hear you thinking, "When two people like each other, it doesn't matter who chases who now does it?" It does. Trust me, it does. Men and women are equal but not alike. You can initiate the conversation, you can flirt, you can leave the door open by helping him a bit, but you cannot chase after him. Ever. Consider it a bad omen.

Men who like you will feel the unstoppable urge to take the next step. The attraction he should feel for you will be that powerful. So when a man doesn't take this step, you'll know he's just not that into you. This is a very important red flag you should never ignore. Your mind will try to rationalize and deny it; it will come up with sentences like "He's probably afraid or rejection or doesn't know that I like him, let me help him a hand" or "These are not the 50s, I can go ahead and ask *him* out." Please don't be fooled.

Relationships are hard enough. If you have to work hard to get him before the relationship has even started, consider that a prediction of a very disturbing and difficult relationship ahead. You might rationalize that he's shy, or that men and women are equal and so it should be fine for you to chase him. It really isn't. Shy men will still go for what they want. They might do it in a nervous way while they're scared to death you will reject them, but they'll still go for it.

And sure, men and women are equal. But this has everything to do with the way nature intends the mating procedure to go. We cannot mess with nature. When we do, problems arise. When you start to chase him, you're more than easy to get. Let me reiterate. When you start to chase him, you're more than easy to get. You won't be valuable to him, even though you might be the most interesting woman he'll ever meet.

The natural procedure hasn't been followed, and as a result, he'll feel something is wrong. The natural procedure most men follow (except for players, narcissists, manipulative men, psychopaths) is very simple:

- Man sees woman he likes (thus, the woman just passed the physical attraction test, since he doesn't know her personality yet).

- Man wants to introduce himself and start talking to her.

- Man gets scared. He thinks about all of the risks and consequences:

    o *She will think I'm too tall/little/overweight/bald/dumb/poor/ugly.*

- o *If she turns me down, I'll feel bad for days, weeks, or even months.*

- o *If someone else, especially someone I know, sees me getting rejected, I'll never get over it.*

- Most men now decide to not follow through on it. Their negative voice has sufficiently scared them. They won't take the risk and do nothing. That's fine. You don't want these men.

- Some men will think: "*I really really want to get to know her better so regardless of the anxiety I'll feel, I'll go for it!*"

That's the guy you want to invest your time and heart in. It's really simple. If a guy doesn't step over his anxiety, come over to introduce himself, flirt with you, or ask you out, he's not interested enough.

And sure, if you then start to flirt with him and take the lead, you might get somewhere since he was at least a bit interested in you. Nevertheless, this guy will lose interest quickly, simply because he didn't have enough of it in the first place. This is a big trap.

And it's a difficult one, I must admit. It's hard to find a great guy; it's hard to find a great guy who's interested in you, and it's even harder to turn your back to him because he wasn't interested enough to ask you out or take the lead himself.

When the price seems so close, it's easy to overlook this natural procedure and go for it just like the kids who ate the marshmallow right away. If you want to follow the strategy with the best long-term future ahead, you'll pick a guy who has jumped over a couple of hurdles before he could get to you. You'll wait to eat the marshmallow.

If he doesn't put in the effort in the early stages of the relationship, he sure won't later. And that's silly, because by that time you will be emotionally invested in him and the relationship and it will hurt.

Let me repeat that the initial stage of the relationship is where he's showing you his best side; he will be putting in the highest effort! If he chooses not to put in the effort to ask you out and take all those first steps, you've just taken a glimpse into the crystal ball of your future. His efforts will only decline from this point on.

You always get the man you've chosen. If you pick a guy who doesn't want to put in a great enough effort to get you, he won't put in an effort to keep you. The woman has the power here. He has to do the grunt work. Please don't go looking for equal rights or equality here. Let him work for it, for you. That's what makes you a high-value woman, and it's the best way to naturally gage his true level of interest in you.

Furthermore men need the challenge of going after you, of putting in the effort, and feeling that excitement. It's crucial. Some women make it way too easy by showing interest too soon or worse, by initiating the chase. Men need to do the initial chasing. Always.

Imagine a guy who's ready to go hunt for a wild boar. He's walking in the woods, wearing special boots he bought online that make as little noise as possible. On top of that, he's wearing camouflage pants and a camouflage jacket. He's not wearing any deodorant so the animals can't smell him from a mile away. His face is covered with some dirt so he blends in nicely into the background. He's well prepared. He has been reading up on this subject, put in a lot of effort, and is ready for the challenge.

Then, after a couple of hours of walking slowly through the woods on a rainy day, there it is, a wild boar. Finally. He swiftly licks his finger and puts it up in the air to figure out what direction the wind is blowing. It's the right direction so the wild boar won't be able to smell him when he closes in. As he slowly takes out his gun and starts to aim, the wild boar looks up and sees him.

"Hey," the wild boar says. "Thanks for making me feel so special! I realize you could have picked any other wild boar, dear, pig, or whatever out there, so I appreciate it. But hey," the wild boar continues. "I think I'm too far away for you to have a great shot. There are a couple of trees standing in between us. Let me make it easier on you. I'll come closer."

The wild boar eagerly trots closer to the hunter. "Is this close enough? Am I in the right position like this? Or should I turn around? Like this? Tell me what you need and I'll do it."

Can you picture this ridiculous scene? Can you imagine how the hunter wouldn't even want to shoot that wild boar? If he wanted to eat some easy meat, some "no effort" meat, he would have bought some in the supermarket. He wouldn't have put in such an effort. The fun, the challenge, and the excitement are gone.

This is exactly what some women do when they ask for *his* number first, when they ask *him* out on a date, when they initiate and take the lead during the dating procedure. It's not the way nature intended it to go.

Please remember the two main reasons:

1. You cannot gauge his interest in you, chances are you're dealing with a guy who's lazy, not sufficiently interested, and you're about to embark on a rocky ride.
2. You're taking away all of his fun and his interest will plummet.

Sandra is one of my coaching clients who had this problem. She was a member of a certain gym and while she was training there, there was a guy who caught her attention. He was looking over and more often than not "accidently" training in her vicinity. One day, he found the courage to walk over and say hi. They had a nice chat. He flirted a bit with Sandra, and she reciprocated. She loved it.

He then took it one step further. He got her name from the front desk, found her LinkedIn profile, and copied her e-mail address from it. He sent her an e-mail to ask her out.

That's almost stalking, if you ask me, but again proof of what a guy goes through when he's really interested.

Sandra said yes, and they had a great first date. He only kissed her on the cheeks at the end. That same evening, Sandra made a first small mistake by texting him and telling him how much she had liked the date.

She called him the next day. They had a nice chat over the phone and Sandra hinted that they should meet up again. So he invited her over for a glass of wine a couple of days later. Sandra, however, forgot to set up the hour they would meet. As that day started, she wondered why he hadn't picked up on that and she decided to text him, "What time do you want me to come over? I look forward to it."

About an hour later, she got a text stating: "I'm so sorry. I totally forgot that I already had plans for today. I'm going to have to postpone this until the end of the month." Sandra was shocked, since the month had only just started. She decided to stay strong and texted back "OK. Have fun and have a great month."

As two days passed without any sign from him, Sandra couldn't keep it together and decided to text him again: "Hey, I know we can't have that glass of wine, but we do need to work out. How about we meet each other in the gym this week?" Two days later, she got a text back: "I'm so sorry, I canceled by membership there, I'm just too busy."

That's when Sandra first reached out to me; she wanted to know when she should text him again and when she should contact him to set up the date for the end of the month where, again, no specific date or time had been set.

This is a prime example of Sandra acting like the wild boar. She found herself a guy who was interested in her; she clearly had passed the physical attraction test as he had gone through great lengths to get to know her. Then Sandra started to fall for this guy way too fast and act super needy, scaring him away instantly. As if that was not enough, she refused to give up and kept going after him.

Imagine the wild boar running after the hunter, as he was walking back to his car empty-handed and let down by the lack of excitement of challenge. Sandra had been blind to the effects of her behavior, which surprised me since she told me this same script had happened often.

Please don't go against the grain for all of the reasons I've mentioned in this chapter. You deserve better results than the ones you will get by ignoring the way nature has intended our "mating process" to go.

Flirting is OK; that's part of the natural procedure. It shows the man that you've noticed him. You can open the door a little, but he's the one who needs to walk through it and ask you out. Most of the initial efforts need to come from him, at least for the first couple of dates. It's an investment he needs to make and a risk he needs to take.

Think of medieval times where the princess was sitting on her throne, while the knights were literally fighting for her attention, love, and respect. I'm not suggesting you should have men compete against each other for you, but it should always be clear to them that you are a princess and that your love, your respect, and especially your time needs to be earned. This will be impossible if you just give it away, if you start to chase him. Your true knight in shining armor will have fought to be able to get to you.

Some women get this theory, apply it, and then take it one step too far. They play (too) hard to get. Playing hard to get will always work better than starting to chase men yourself, but it's not the best strategy. I've coached women who couldn't find a guy because they had a list of 'required qualities' that virtually no man could ever live up to. And even if he did, they didn't keep him around long enough to ever find out. Really, I've met women who take being a high-value woman a couple of steps too far.

There's a fine equilibrium that requires experimentation. You may often leave the door open a little bit, but it's always clear the man needs to step through it. That's his job. Men do the picking; women do the choosing. Men have to risk rejection and chase women. Then the women decide whether they want to accept him or not.

Please take a moment to reflect on what part of the spectrum you're currently positioned. When you fall for a guy or are interested in a guy, how easy do you make it on him? To what extent do you initiate the important mating steps in the early stages of the relationship?

Trap Five: How a Guy falls for You

Jenny is one of my clients, and she had an interesting problem with Ron. She met Ron at a company party where the two of them hit it off. Ron had introduced himself to her, and it was clear that he was flirting with her.

What Jenny couldn't understand was why he was not asking for her number, or any way to contact her. Sure, they worked for the same company, but it was a large company. Chances were they'd never meet again. As the evening progressed, Jenny's feelings started to grow more and more. She was flustered and for some reason loved everything about Ron.

Then at some point Ron said: "I loved our talk Jenny, I hope I will see you again but I have to go home now. Take care".

Jenny was flabbergasted and a little bit mad at herself for not mustering up the courage to ask for his phone number. "What now?" she thought.

The next day, during her lunch break, she decided to look through the company employee's list. Ron had been wearing a badge the night before, so she knew his last name. And lo and behold, she found Ron. His picture was just as she remembered him. A handsome man with deep blue eyes and a look full of self-confidence. After some pondering, Jenny decided to send Ron an e-mail. She just wanted to thank him for the great conversation, nothing more, although she was hoping that more could come from it. It took Ron about 24 hours to respond, but he did.

They kept e-mailing back and forth for a couple of weeks and still Ron didn't ask her out. Jenny didn't get it. That's when she contacted me for some coaching. All I could do is explain to Jenny that Ron was, for some reason, not interested in her. There's probably nothing she could have done to change his opinion, and that's OK. We're not compatible with every single person we happen to like.

Jenny had stepped into one of the more classic traps here. She was waiting for Ron to fall for her. She hoped her witty e-mail conversations would eventually lead to him asking her out. And, in theory, that could happen if Ron had enough feelings and attraction for her to begin with.

But that's not the point I want to make here. Some women believe men can fall in love slowly. They don't. Men fall hard and fast, never soft and slow. Men almost instantly decide whether they want to be with a woman or not. Not long after, they will decide whether she's wife material or not so much.

That first part of the decision- making process is important. If he doesn't decide "Whoa, that's a woman I want to be with" during the first 10-20 minutes of conversation, he never will. Men really are that superficial. Men don't become friends first, only to fall for you later. There are men who seem to do this, but that's only because they didn't have the courage to openly flirt with you earlier. Becoming friends first is the wimpy guy's strategy. I'm not pointing fingers here; I've used this strategy too as a young teenager.

Ron flirted with Jenny which proved he was somewhat interested. But probably not too much or he would have asked for her number. And even if he, for some reason, couldn't find the courage then, he surely would have when Jenny contacted him again. This was her way of opening the door a little bit. He should have stepped through at that point but didn't.

I've seen so many women wait for a guy to fall for them and this is a mistake. There are so many men out there, great men you won't have to wait for. Men who would take charge and go after you, because you're worth it.

Men and women are different here. Some women need time before they fall in love with a guy; it can sometimes take them months before they'll start to feel attracted to a guy and fall deeply in love with him. Men are much quicker. So please, never wait for a guy to see the light. Men often change their mind from "interested" to "not so interested" for a myriad of reasons. Sadly, that isn't a two-way street. When a man's interest level is not high enough to go after you in the beginning, it won't ever raise to a level high enough that you can have a fulfilled relationship with him.

Trap Six: Your Most Important Bargaining Chip

Men are driven by success, money, and procreation. You might not be able to influence the first two, but you sure can influence the third pillar in his life.

Men need sex. When given the choice between all the money in the world or the ability to have sex with anyone they want in the world, most men will go for option two. Nevertheless, should the genie in the bottle grant wish number two, men will get sick and tired of the abundance. It will start to lose value. But that's not the point here. Men need sex. It really is that simple. It's an absolute need that's really high on their list.

Strange things happen to a man when he's not able to be sensual and sexual with a woman. If masturbation is taken away, he would go crazy. His urges and frustration would rise so high that he would eventually lose it and position having sex as a top priority on his to do list, whatever the consequences would be.

Geoffrey Miller Ph.D., evolutionary professor at the University of New Mexico and author of an interesting book called the *Mating Mind,* says that almost every action a man takes is to reach one specific goal: get noticed by women and eventually, get women.

According to Geoffrey, the car men buy, the job they choose, the high salary they want, the clothes they wear...everything they do serves one goal: getting the attention of the opposite sex.

I want to debunk an important myth here that claims that most men think about sex every six seconds. They really don't. They think about success, entrepreneurship, career, income, cars, etc. They need all of these to become successful, so they can be more attractive to as many women as possible and to eventually get sex. In fact, men always think about sex, not just every six seconds.

Women are different. Most women I've met, interviewed, dated, or coached have loved sex, but they didn't *need* it as much as men do. A lack of having sex wouldn't force them to surf the Internet in search of porn, to call a hotline and talk to a sexy voice about sex, to take someone out to dinner and try to impress her, or to call someone to give them sex in exchange for money. Most men need sex so badly, they will pick at least one of these to get some satisfaction. It's a true urge that most women won't understand.

I do realize there are exceptions. I've met women who had a strong sex drive that could easily keep up with men, but I bet it still wasn't their primary motivator.

Sex is valuable to a man. Please don't give it away too easily. Please don't reward his bad behavior by giving him sex when he's not behaving the way you'd like, and don't use it in an effort to seduce him or make him fall for you. It's your most important bargaining chip.

I'm not asking you to use it as one. It's never OK to have to play games to keep a guy in your life. But giving him your body too soon can and will decrease your value. Giving your body when he's not behaving the way you'd like will lower how valuable you are to him.

Men like to chase you, to conquer you. A great way to keep the relationship interesting for him is to make him work to get you physically, even when you're already in a long-term relationship with him. Men always go after what they cannot get. Since you shouldn't be playing hard to get, even though it will always work better than being easy to get, it's best to not make it self-evident. Keep it challenging.

This sounds silly, even ridiculous. However, never forget men are totally different creatures compared to women. They are wired in a different way.

Many women have asked me, "Sure, but if I wait with sex or make sex a bit harder to get, won't he leave me?"

That is a possibility. But it's a great way to weed out the bad guys, the ones who indeed just wanted to have sex and cannot see further than your body. Unfortunately, some men just want to play games with you. It's important to test them, to throw some challenges at them and see who sticks around. Those interested in more than your body will wait and continue to pursue you.

I had a private coaching client in a committed relationship with a guy who had an extremely high libido. He wanted to have sex every single day. She told him she believed 3-4 times per week would be enough to which he responded, "Well, before I met you I went to a special club with friends. Only men are allowed into that club. There are women present, and you can have intercourse with them. If you can't give me enough sex, I'll need to go back to that club."

What a club. She asked me what to do. Sure, to us, the answer is pretty clear: NEXT. But to her, it wasn't; she was blinded by love, as it often is the case.

Sex had become a commodity in their relationship. He forgot the value of her body, of being with her, and as a result, he was even prepared to be totally rude to her and blackmail her.

As I dug a bit deeper, her mistake happened earlier on in the relationship. She fell for him pretty soon after meeting him, and they had sex after their first date. It apparently was a romantic moment, even movie-like. But it turned out she didn't know anything about his true intentions before she gave herself to him. And that was wrong for two reasons:

1. Your hormones do funny things as soon as you're intimate with a guy.

I love the natural equilibrium and flow of things. But nature can play games with us too. Nature doesn't know we have contraception. So it's fairly simple, nature thinks, "When a man and a woman have sex, a baby is possibly made."

It's as simple as that. Babies need to be fed, protected, educated, and so on for multiple years. So it's best that the father sticks around. It's also best for the mother to not start to dislike the father for any reason since she might then think, "I don't need you, I can make it on my own." Nature doesn't know we've evolved away from this in the last 20-30 years. Women don't *need* a man any longer, but nature still thinks we live in a dangerous setting where we can be attacked by predators and dangerous creatures any given moment.

Our evolution found a great solution for this. The woman should fall madly in love with a man during the baby-making process. That's why and how she will tolerate his weird behavior and will stick around. When a woman is pregnant, she should stay around her man, the father of the baby. To get there, nature has created lots of different hormones, like oxytocin, that bond you to your man (and to your newborn baby later on, since it's best you don't dislike that baby either and want to keep caring for her or him).

Oxytocin is the empathy and bonding hormone; it will bond you to whoever you're with when it is released. It doesn't know the difference between you having sex with your husband of five years or a guy you met last night. This hormone is the main reason why most women let their guard down and want to bond after having sex.

When a man has an orgasm, however, dopamine is released. That is his dominant hormone. Dopamine is the pleasure hormone that gives a feeling of achievement, of victory.

Dr. Loretta Graziano Breuning Ph.D. once explained in *Psychology Today* that oxytocin is the very reason why some women fall for bad boys. Most women link that oxytocin release to feelings that say, "This is your perfect partner. This person is trustworthy." This, according to Breuning, is merely an illusion.

As soon as you let a man touch you intimately, your body knows you're about to have sex. And having sex with a man equals a big possibility of conceiving a baby. All those hormones are then released to make you bond with and to that man. You'll fall in love with him.

Isn't this strange? Have you ever felt this? The minute you have sex with a guy, you start to care more about him. You start to develop more feelings for him. Now you know the science behind this. Explain this system to yourself the next time you're about to fall into the trap of becoming intimate too soon. And if it's too late, realize it's not love yet, it's just oxytocin.

2. You won't know his true intentions when you give away sex too soon.

When you have sex too soon, you might fall for him because of the oxytocin and other chemical reactions. Love can make you blind; it will let you rationalize some of his not-so-perfect behaviors. It will then be significantly harder to see his true intentions because of all of the hormones and resulting special emotions you'll feel and because you gave him what he wanted too soon.

He might have just been looking for sex, not a committed relationship. It's possible you are fine with that, but in case you're not, there's no way to find out his true intentions at this time. Men who are only interested in sex won't be willing to wait. So try to wait at least a couple of dates before you have sex with a guy, as a test. See who sticks around and continues to treat you like a princess.

You'll know he's worthy of you by looking at his actions. Does he keep his promises? Does he behave like a good man around you?

This last question is an interesting one. A good man who has good plans with you will want to provide and protect. He's built to do that; it's in his genes. He will always want to protect his special one. Is he doing that? Does he try to take care of you? When you're sick, does he come over to care for you? When you have a handyman task to be performed in the house, does he take care of it for you? These are important clues.

Guys who are only interested in sleeping with you will always keep their investment to a minimum -- the minimum they need to do to get your body. That's it. Guys who are truly into you will go above and beyond. Not because they have to, they'll do it because they want to. That's the reason why it's best to wait for sex. It will force him to show his true intentions.

Trap Seven: Not behaving or feeling like a high value woman

The high-value woman is independent, strong, emotionally stable, happy with herself and her life, and most importantly, unwavering in the standard of behavior she requires from men. When a man does something she does not like, she won't punish him by giving him the silent treatment, getting mad, or by nagging; she will simply give him less of her time and attention, because she has better things to do.

These characteristics make a woman very attractive to most men. It also makes her bulletproof against the type of men who prey on women. Men who treat women badly are like water; they always look for the path with the least resistance. They try to put in minimum time to get a maximum return. High-value women never give them a positive ROI because they look right through their BS.

Low-value women are different. I'm sure you're not part of this group, but I do want to elaborate a bit since the low-value woman will continue to attract the wrong kind of guy. Low-value women often have low self-esteem and simply don't realize their worth. They don't know they have certain powers over men. They think the only power tools at their disposal are jealousy, nagging, and anger. They try to manipulate men into behaving the way they want to. It's the only way they know to get what they want. Nevertheless they still fail to see that this never ever works in the long term.

Instead, they repel men because of their low-value behavior. Here are some examples:

1. When a man is disrespectful and gives an explanation or excuse that sounds reasonable, the woman accepts it and believes it won't happen again.
2. Low-value women forgive easily.
3. They believe his words.
4. They often believe *he* can get better, so they need to keep him close.
5. They believe they aren't a high-value woman since this value is based on looks or something else they don't have.
6. Low-value women are clingy, needy, and emotionally unstable. Being with them is like walking through a minefield every day. You never know when the next one will go off.

These women need some simple mind-shifts that are easy to explain and a bit harder to implement. It's worth it. The trick is to mimic some of the mindsets and behaviors of the high-value woman.

Increase Your Perceived Value

High-value women have a life of their own, and they keep it that way during relationships. They're often so busy they don't even want a guy. The crucial difference between high- and low-value women is the low value woman might have her own activities, friends, and hobbies. But as soon as she meets a guy she falls for, she will start to raise his value above the value of whatever was important to her in the past. He becomes number one, her only source of pleasure and fulfillment. They lose focus and get tunnel vision. They can only see *him*. This is not always their fault; nature has its way of changing their emotions (oxytocin and so on) to make him the top priority in her life. High-value women suffer from these hormones as well, but they consciously decide to steer clear of the consequences.

We've already seen that you can decide to step away from some of your basic instincts. This is often a good idea when it comes to relationships and love. There are two main reasons:

1. You deserve a full life. Even the greatest guy in the world cannot provide you with everything you need and should experience. Focusing on him and revolving everything around him will make it easier to fall in a deep black hole whenever the relationship goes awry or whenever he wants to spend a weekend away with his friends.
2. You won't be pushing him away. Men will find it hard to fear commitment, to feel suffocated when their girlfriend or wife has a life of her own. This is further explained later in this book.

Some simple extra techniques to behave like a high-value woman are:

1. Take a while to get back to him. When he calls you and you miss the call, don't call back right away. Finish what you started first. When he texts, take a while to answer him. The less interested he seems, the more disrespectful he is, the longer it should take you to get back to him.
2. Be busy. When he always assumes your calendar will be free whenever he asks you out, especially when he calls for last-minute

dates often. Tell him you have other plans even if you don't.

3. Have other things to do. When talking on the phone, using video chat, or any other form of direct communication, be the first to leave the conversation because you have stuff to do.

4. Whenever he did something you really don't like, especially something that is disrespectful, lower his value. Be busy and plan even more activities with other people. If you find this step difficult, write down a list of his negative traits. Focus on his negative traits to help you remove the blindfolds that love might have put on.

High-value women are not perfect! They make mistakes, feel pain, and often have to consciously control their emotions. They would love to get instant gratification just like anybody else, but they decide to control their emotions since they want to control the long-term consequences of their actions. When you control your emotions, you control your future! Sounds spiritual, but if you haven't done this, please give it a try. You'll be pleased with the results. Whenever you feel an unwanted emotion, ask yourself: "if I act upon this emotion, what will then be the long-term consequences of it?". Then decide what's best for you.

Drop him when he's not living up to your (necessary) expectations.

I've met and coached countless women waiting for someone to become the man they've always wanted. They waited around for him to get his act together, for him to realize she was the one, for him to find a job, for him to stop fooling around, and more.

These women waited in vain. While their mind and hearts where busy with Mr. Loser, they forgot to see the true value of all the other great men they'd met or could have met. Love gives you selective vision; it can sometimes even blind you. You won't see the other great men even when they're presented on a silver platter as long as you're stuck with a guy who is never going to turn into the man you deserve. This is especially true when you have sex with him. One of the other side effects of oxytocin is that it makes you solely focus on that one special person.

The high-value woman knows this and is not afraid to dump him when she realizes they have no future together. Men don't change. If there are some things you could not possibly live with, it's time to walk away. You'll be thanking yourself later.

Trap Eight: Opposites Attract

You've heard that opposites attract. It's true. However, it doesn't mean it's necessarily a good thing. During my many years as a relationship coach, I've seen countless people who were not supposed to be together, joining each other on a never-ending emotional rollercoaster ride from hell.

The most simplistic example involves the good woman falling for a bad guy who clearly doesn't treat her well. She knows it but can't help her attraction. She craves his kindness and affection, and the couple of minutes he does give it every now and then are enough to keep her waiting for more. It takes a lot of courage to break free from that magnetism. For some, it's impossible.

Codependent women, who had a bad childhood where love was unsure and unpredictable (Daddy loves me; Daddy loves me not), often fall for men who are narcissistic, manipulative, and treat them badly. This is not by accident. Freud believed that we seem to go for what's familiar. Ridiculous as that sounds, women who had a bad father will go for a bad man. Women who had an all-demanding narcissistic father will fall for narcissistic men even though they know better. This is true for many types of partner we can pick. People with an anxious attachment style often fall for people with an avoidant attachment style. Messy people often fall for someone who likes to keep things clean.

Multiple subconscious forces are at play here. Some stem from our childhood; others stem from aspiration. A lazy guy can fall for a successful woman because he hopes she can turn things around for him.

These are all examples of opposites that attract. The trap? This magnetic attraction is caused by the challenge, by the emotional rollercoaster itself and not by love.

At least one of the parties in these couples is trying to change the other's thinking. We of course know it won't change. The successful woman waits for her lazy loser boyfriend to get his act together and start working on his career; the kind and sweet woman hopes her bad guy will see the light and start treating her with the respect she deserves somewhere in the future. Some people keep stepping into this trap, as they keep attracting or feeling attracted to the wrong kind of partner.

If you ever fell into this trap, it's crucial to know that the attraction you are feeling is not love. Love is not about magnetic *tension* between two people; love is about a deep will to care for each other, to be there for each other, to be a team. I'm not stating two opposites cannot love each other. I just want you to realize that the feelings of the "Does he love me? Does he not?" is not love. It's a very basic and simple attraction caused by the opposite poles of a magnet.

Trap Nine: "The One"

You enter very dangerous grounds the moment you crown someone "the one." This is the moment you are giving away your power. While this moment should be carefully chosen and reviewed, some women give this seal or crown away way too easily.

If you've read any of my other books then you already know I'm not a fan of the "only one" concept. There are multiple soul mates for you. If we look at percentages, there are a lot more men out there you won't be compatible with, who don't deserve your attention, your love, and your time. But there still are a ton of guys with whom you could have a very fulfilling relationship.

Some women overlook a man's flaws and incompatibilities, decide he's the one, and stop looking for someone better. This is an understandable reaction. Looking around and trying to find your life partner is one of the hardest things to do. It feels like a true mission impossible.

Men face this challenge, too. As a man, I have to muster up the courage to walk over to a woman and ask for her phone number (rejection possibility one). Call her and ask her out (rejection possibility two). Find something cool and interesting to do on out first date. Try to kiss her at the end of the first or second date (rejection possibility three). Continue dating her, spend time with her, and so on. Eventually we may move in together. Most often moving in together allows you to really see whether you're compatible or not. The other person can no longer hide their flaws, mood swings, bad habits, and so on. It can seem like a good idea to keep giving it a try after all that initial investment, doesn't it?

When you're dating, you see the best side of the other person. That's clear. If, during the dating stage, you see any bad habits or personality traits you cannot live with, get out of there. This is the other person at his best. It will only get worse.

Just like anyone else, I've had relationships where it took me months before I realized we were not that good of a fit. That's the moment where you decide there are fundamental flaws in the other person that aren't compatible with you. What can you do then? If you decide to break up, you've got to come to terms with the fact that you've wasted hours, days, months, or sometimes even years of your life. And who knows, you might never find anyone better!

And that's the trap! Women who crown "the one" too soon will not be able to avoid this trap. They might not see his shortcomings because of the blindness that comes with love or worse, they will be in a part of Egypt called Denial. They will decide to overlook the major challenges and come up with excuses. When they finally decide it won't get any better they have to realize they've wasted months or years waiting for it to change.

A couple of strong under-the-radar forces cause this denial. Here are some examples:

1. Love makes them blind.
2. They're afraid to be alone again.
3. They cannot come to terms with the fact they've wasted their time.
4. They believe his promises to change.
5. They lie to themselves and say it's not that big of a deal.

6. They believe they can change him.
7. They allow those sporadic good moments to be enough to stick around.

The title of "the one" should be earned and not given away too soon. It should only be given to the man with whom you want to spend the rest of your life, <u>even though he will never ever change</u>. You like him just the way he is.

Trap Ten: The Wrong Man

As I mentioned earlier, finding the right guy is quite the predicament. It takes time, and the interview process is not an easy one. This next trap is all about falling for the wrong man, which I'm sure has happened to almost every woman in the dating world.

Some women know he has some traits that make him the wrong man but decide to wait it out and see if he changes. Some women started off great but then have a revelation deep into the relationship.

Some good men will pick up bad behavior as you go through your journey together. Anything that emasculates him -- the loss of a job, the failure of a business venture -- might make him depressed, negative, alcoholic, etc.

Most men, however, do not change and will have had that bad behavior from the beginning. The women who date them have simply decided to overlook his obvious flaws or hope it will change one day. Some women put up with bad behavior because they are confident it will change.

It won't.

We all need to be more honest toward ourselves, step out of denial, and decide to see things clearly. If you look back at past relationships that ended badly, you'll notice that his flaws were obvious in the early stages of the relationship, often even sooner.

I've had my fair share of this as well. The first girl I ever dated started to make me unhappy after the two-week mark of the relationship. She told me how much she was attracted to me, how much she loved me, and how much she wanted to be with me. My gut feeling, however, was communicating an entirely different story. I could tell something was wrong, and I had difficulties focusing and concentrating on other things. I was still going to the university at that time, and this negatively impacted my grades. Eight months into the relationship, she ended it. Two years later, I found out she was a lesbian. And apparently a pretty good actress, too. She couldn't fool my gut instincts, however. I should have listened to them. Her flaws in our relationship were obvious, but I had chosen to overlook them.

This has happened twice more, and it has made me waste a lot of time in each of those relationships. The other women had personality disorders that I quickly picked up on. I, however, foolishly believed it would pass or that I, being a coach who helps people change, would be able to change them. I was wrong.

I knew these women weren't right for me before the two-month mark. It usually only takes a couple of weeks of dating to conclude that something is wrong. At that point, I should have asked myself, "When you've just bought a brand new car and a red, unknown light starts to flash on the dashboard before you're on the highway, what do you do? Do you continue to drive into the sunset or do you go return the car?" This sounds pretty harsh, I know. Our partners are not cars; they are emotional beings and so are we. It hurts each and every time you get dumped or when you yourself have to end a relationship. But you understand the sentiment. **This trap is clear. It's about falling for the wrong person, realizing it, and despite everything, deciding to continue to give it shot after shot after shot.**

When you look at your own life or the lives of the people you know, how many of them have stepped into this trap? Most of us have, and that's OK. The question is how many more times will we step into the trap with our eyes wide open, knowing it will hurt somewhere down the line?

Getting back together with an ex is a side trap of this main trap. Many women decide to give it another try with their ex because they prefer to not be alone. They miss the bond they had with that person; they miss the excitement (both the highs and the lows of the emotional rollercoaster), or most importantly, because he promised them it would be different this time. It never is.

I've statistically counted all of my coaching clients who ever decided to get back together with an ex. Not a single one of those couples have survived the five-year mark after getting back together. The reason is pretty simple. The relationship went south the first time for a reason, and this very reason will resurface pretty quickly.

When you decide he's not the right guy, for any reason, take off the blinders and try to imagine living the rest of your life with him while he remains exactly the same. That's probably an accurate simulation of the future.

But how do you know you're dealing with the wrong guy? I'll deal with some of the types of really 'bad' guys later on, but for now, here are some red flags you should look out for.

1. How does he deal with problems and challenges? People often show their true persona when things don't go to plan. How does he treat you and others?

Whenever he's facing a large obstacle it's OK for him to be in a bad mood. We all might be. Examples of large obstacles include losing a job, losing a client, any form of income loss, getting bad news, and so on. This is, however, never a reason for him to treat you without respect. There's never a reason for a man to disrespect a woman when she's respectful toward him. If you see him treating you or anyone else badly when he faces a large obstacle, consider that a red flag.

Some men, however, will already get in a bad mood when something small goes wrong. They get the wrong dish in a restaurant, they don't get the table they wanted, the waiter wasn't friendly, they got stuck in a traffic jam, etc. When these make him lose his balance, consider that a major red flag. Life throws obstacles at us all the time. It's never easy, for anyone. You'll have your own problems to deal with and battles to fight, and if he gets upset over these little things, chances are he'll be a nightmare to be around whenever a major challenge or obstacle arrives. These might even be signs he suffers from a major personality disorder like borderline or narcissism. These men are to be avoided.

If you've not seen this type of man (lucky you), you've seen him in movies. They are the guys who smack their fist into a mirror whenever something goes wrong, who throw their phone at the ground, who lose their temper when anything doesn't go to plan or how they wanted it. Some people blame others and the world whenever something goes wrong. They get mad at everyone but fail to realize they are the ones who can fix it or at least caused it. These men often become dictators in the relationship.

He needs to be able to laugh it off and deal with the challenge without getting mad or upset. These are the solution-seekers instead of complainers. These are the men with emotional intelligence, the men who will be able to protect you and form a team with you when life throws one of its many challenges. What group does your guy belong to?

2. Is he part of the team? Does he enhance the quality of your life? When you get some attitude and objectively look at your relationship, is he improving the quality of your life with or by his actions? Not because he makes you feel good when he says "I love you," but is he truly helping you to move forward in life? Does he help you without you needing to ask it? When you're sick, does he stand by your side and help you? All normal men want to protect and care for their woman. If you don't see this treat in him then he a. doesn't like you enough or b. isn't a normal guy...

3. Is he afraid to hurt your feelings? This is an important and a tricky one. You deserve an authentic guy who will be upfront with you. Whenever he hurts your feelings because he's disrespectful, he should lose a whole lot of points. Whenever he hurts you because he's honest, authentic, and telling you the truth, he should gain points.

Here's a simple example: You're getting ready for a night out. You ask him what he thinks of your dress. Politely, he tells you that he isn't too fond of it and prefers the red dress you wore last time. He could have lied to not upset you, but he chose to be authentic and tell you the truth. This is an important quality.

A player and most forms of men who play games would have chosen to avoid any turmoil. Men who are not authentic and honest about the little things will definitely not be about the larger things.

Positive reinforcement is a dangerous part of this trap, too. Many behavioral tests have been done on pigeons and rats to explain and explore human behavior. Famous psychologists like B.F Skinner (Harvard) even taught pigeons how to play Ping-Pong. One of the experiments with pigeons can give us some powerful insights when it comes to staying in a bad relationship. Pigeon One was put in a cage with a lever. Each time the pigeon pushed the lever some food was given. It doesn't take the pigeon long to figure this out. Whenever it's hungry, it pushes the lever and gets some food. This pigeon feels very secure about getting food and has no worries. This is a clear example of positive reinforcement.

Then the researchers stop giving food when the lever is pushed. Pigeon One tries to push the lever a couple of times, sees there's no food coming and decides, "Good times are over; this lever doesn't give me any food any longer. I'm sure of that since it was very consistent before. Pushing meant food. Now I change that into: pushing means nothing." Pigeon One is fine with that and starts to look elsewhere for food. It stops pushing the lever.

Pigeon Two is treated differently. It's put in the exact same type of cage with a lever. The only difference is pushing the lever only sporadically gives food. Pigeon Two, for example, pushes the lever three times and only gets food the fourth time. Then it pushes it two times and gets food right away. The next time it takes eleven pushes before some food is given. Then the researchers stop giving food when the lever is pushed.

Pigeon Two frantically keeps pushing the lever as a result. It thinks, "I shouldn't give up. This has happened before. It happens all the time; I keep putting in an effort and get nothing in return. I should keep trying since this lever is erratic, food should still come if I keep pushing. I just don't know when that will be."

Pigeon Two eventually gets a full burn-out and falls down from exhaustion. It had continued to push the lever, endlessly, when no food came out of it. Pigeon Two had lost its mind.

I love animals, and I don't condone this test...or any testing on animals. But I think we can learn a lot from this experiment. Can you see how the experiment relates to falling for the wrong partner?

When you fall for the right man, his behavior should remain stable. Should it ever change in the future (e.g., he starts to respect you less), you'll know it's time to go; it's easy. It's not working out. When he goes from being respectful all the time to being disrespectful, you'll know it's over.

Women who fall for the wrong guy are quickly put into the position of Pigeon Two. His affection and love is given sporadically, and she has no idea when it will come. She tries to be a good, loving woman; she's there for him and ready to help him out wherever she can (thus pushing the lever). He, on the other hand, only gives some affection, some love every now and then and she never knows when.

Whenever his behavior turns into bad behavior, however long this lasts, she keeps hoping for things to get better. She knows there's a good guy in there somewhere (just as Pigeon Two had learned the lever does give food every now and then). This woman will continue to rationalize his lack of love and respect. She thinks, "I shouldn't give up. This has happened before. It happens all the time that I keep putting in an effort and get nothing in return. I should keep trying since he is erratic, his love and affection should still come if I keep trying. I just don't know when that will be."

At the end, she burns out, gets depressed, or suffers from any other form of mental break down as a consequence. Some women get trapped into this loop for years or even decades.

If you're ever trapped in a relationship that resembles the cage of Pigeon Two, where what you need (love, attention, affection) is only given sporadically. Be wary and try to understand this erratic positive reinforcement is dangerous. Call it quits before your mind or body calls it quits on you.

Trap Eleven: The MANipulator

This trap is closely related to the previous traps, yet it is an important one to mention. I will spare you the psychological theories and experiments, but Freud already said we usually end up with someone who resembles our parent of the opposite sex. Multiple studies have proven this.

We have already discussed this, but just reiterate: women who had a bad father often end up falling for bad guys. It's as if they are magnetically attracted to these bad boys; they simply cannot get away from it. If their father was a narcissist, chances are the men they end up with will also be narcissists who demand obedience.

Some men are true manipulators. I discuss them in my other book *Red Flags, Signs He's Playing Games With You*. These are the men who consciously use manipulative strategies to string you along. Some of these men are so good at it that their women don't even notice it.

For this trap, however, I specifically talk about women who know they deserve better but choose to stay in that relationship because they're attracted to that bad guy like a moth to a flame. It literally hurts every time they get too close.

Most manipulators have a mental disorder. If you ever have to deal with a pure manipulator who tries to change your behavior and sometimes your personality, chances are you're dealing with a narcissist or someone with a borderline personality disorder. Borderlines are people who see life in black and white. Gray does not exist. They either feel really good or really bad. And when they feel bad, all hell breaks lose. They will feel very bad emotionally and totally empty inside; they won't be able to deal with it. Everyone close to them gets the blame. The closer you are to him, the stronger he will lash out.

Beth, one of my clients, explains:

When John had entered in what I called the border zone, it was as if a demon or someone else had taken over. My once so lovable husband was gone, at least for a while. I was to blame for everything. Dinner wasn't prepared to his liking; I should have ironed his shirts in some other way. He told me I was ugly or fat (even though I'm not) and more. This should be enough of a reason to leave him. But when John was in a good mood, he was the best husband I could ever wish for. He would buy me flowers, be kind, call me his princess, kiss me in a very passionate way, and behave exactly like my Prince Charming would.

So I could see there was good in him too. Most often he was good. Nevertheless, I always felt as if I was walking on eggshells. I never knew when I would step upon another landmine and unleash the rage in him."

What Beth explains here is very typical for someone with a borderline personality disorder. Her mistake is believing that she's triggering his rages by stepping on a so-called landmine. Although I'm not a psychologist, this is a subject I'm very devoted to since one of my girlfriends (and not by accident, my own mother) suffered from this personality disorder. When someone with a borderline personality disorder feels bad -- and they can feel bad for any reason under the sun -- they feel so bad they want to explode. If you're standing close and say anything at all that gives them a bad feeling on top of what they're already experiencing, explode they will and the entire blast will be directed at you.

The most important takeaway is that it is not your fault. People with a borderline personality disorder have had some really negative experiences growing up, causing their personalities to be malformed. This is a true disorder, a true mental disease. People with this disorder will behave in ways that make absolutely no sense since their inner worlds are totally different than ours.

It's not up to you to fix it. You cannot fix it.

The narcissist suffers from a similar disorder. He believes he is the center of the universe. What you might not know, however, is that his behavior stems from a well-covered fear of not being enough, of not being liked. A narcissist will manipulate you because he wants to feel important. Everything has to be his way; other people have to live up to his expectations. This guy will manipulate you and might bully you because that's his way of feeling loved and important. This is a sick way of filling his needs.

If you belong to the caretaker or codependent group of people, then borderlines and narcissists will be very dangerous for you. They will continue to attract and repel you and can make you waste your entire love life. You'll want to fix them, help them, take care of them, etc. The return on your investment, however, will be negative. Be wary of this trap and take steps to remove yourself from the manipulators.

Trap Twelve: Say "No" to Nagging

I can't write a book about the traps in a relationship without writing a chapter about nagging. To this day, I still see so many women who use nagging as their primary weapon to change a man's behavior.

This never works. Ever.

Nagging will only get you positive short-term results. He will change and adapt his behavior just to escape the constant nagging. He will, however, start to lower his interest level in you. And in the long term, all his bad behaviors will start to resurface because there was no intrinsic motivation for him to change. He just wanted to avoid the nagging, not because he decided to change his behavior.

There are much better ways to get him to do things or to make small changes. I deliberately mention small changes because, in the end, people don't change. Many women love to watch those flip-flop renovation projects on television. A couple buys a rundown house and then transforms it into a super home they can sell for a profit or live in themselves.

If you haven't already learned, men are not renovation projects. Even though you could theoretically manage to flip them, they will surely flop back to their old ways later.

That said, when you want him to change a small behavior, use the high-value-woman approach. Talk to him in a sweet, assertive, and sexy way, and state what's important to you. Say, "Honey, it's important to me that you _____."
Try to avoid saying, "Honey can you please _____" or "Honey why don't you ever_____." That would give him

the power. You are not asking for his majesty's approval. Simply state your instructions to him in a sexy but assertive way. It will do wonders, as you'll see.

Not every man will respond. Some men just don't care enough. If you need to nag or get mad in order for him to behave how you wish, it's time to seriously think about the relationship and in most cases, move on.

Even a good guy can be blind to your needs. He won't telepathically see what you want or what is important to you. You'll have to explain it to him. When you communicate what's important to you in a sexy and assertive way (and by sexy, I mean with your sweet voice combined with the pet name you have for him), he should at least start to put in an effort. All good relationships need work and loads of effort from both parties. A good guy will gladly put in the effort. The relationship will feel like a balanced equilibrium of give and take. That's how it's supposed to be.

Trap Thirteen: A Subject to Avoid

I've explained that sex is important to men. You didn't need me for that. As a result, it's crucial that he thinks you are sexy. And yet, this is exactly where so many women make mistakes.

When he sleeps with you and he's clearly aroused, you have passed the physical attraction test. He thinks you're sexy. Most women have insecurities about certain parts of their bodies or in some cases their bodies as a whole. That's fine. I think we all want to improve or change some aspect of our physical appearance.

Some women keep those desires to themselves, and this is a wise choice. Others feel the need to talk about their insecurities with their boyfriends or husbands. They think, "If he's my soul mate, we should be able to talk about everything." That may be true, but I suggest avoiding this topic altogether. Here's why: it lowers your sexual value.

When a woman continues to complain about not being happy with her breasts or any other part of her body, it will be hard for him to still be turned on by it. On top of that, whenever he focuses his attention on a body part she's not happy with, she will cringe and her behavior will change. Her insecurities will surface. An insecure woman is the exact opposite of a sexy woman.

There are two reasons why you should avoid it. If and when you change, cringe, lose your self-esteem, or change your aura in any other way during sex, you break the sexual tension and kill the mood. Let him enjoy your body, even the parts you might not like. If your behavior changes when he starts to focus on the parts you don't like, you start to program and condition him to no longer pay attention to them. If your behavior changes, the mood gets killed. That's exactly what ruins everything at that time for him. Being intimate will become less fun for him; it'll become something to avoid and something that won't arouse him anymore. Can you see what a self-fulfilling prophecy this is?

Discussing your physical insecurities with your man will make him focus on your imperfections. It might take off his blinders and make him see that part of you is indeed imperfect. This sounds silly, but I've had this happen to me personally. One of my previous girlfriends didn't like her legs. This was a challenge since I love legs more than breasts or any other part of the female body. Her continuous negative attention to her legs made me start to dislike her legs more and more. She was programming me to dislike her legs by constantly complaining about them.

We're all human beings; we all have our insecurities. You can talk about any insecurity you want, but when it's a part of your body that he likes and is aroused by, please don't talk about it in a negative way. This will slowly but surely start to condition him, and he will lose interest in you.

That's a self-fulfilling prophecy that will force you to conclude, "See, I was right. That part of me *is* ugly..." It wasn't at first, but you unconsciously programmed him to see it that way.

Trap Fourteen: Actions over Words

Not all men are game players. It nevertheless often is difficult to separate the bad men from the good, especially if you choose to believe what he says. That's why I always stress how it's crucial to mind his actions and not listen to his words.

Men can say and tell you things they don't mean without feeling guilty about it. Not all men do it, of course, but you'll only be able to tell by looking at his actions. Words are easy and require no effort; actions are much more difficult to fake. A man can say, "I love you, and I want to be with you forever" while his actions are proving the opposite.

One action to always examine is his investment in you and your relationship. The rule is simple: Men who are not interested in you will invest the absolute minimum amount of time, attention, and affection to still get what they want from you. This can be your attention, sex, someone to talk to, someone to take out so they don't have to dine alone, and so on.

If he tells you he loves you and his actions, his investment, seem to prove it, you're golden. If you on the other hand notice inconsistencies or your gut feeling is telling you he might not be as honest as he looks, it's time to bottom-line his actions. What's the amount of effort he puts in when it comes to dating you or being with you? Is he chasing you? Do you have the feeling that you're always the one who initiates contact or that you're the one putting in more effort than he is?

Chances are your mind will start to play tricks with you too and will begin to rationalize and find excuses: "I'm sure he's just busy", "I'm sure he had a bad day at work, that's why he....". And sure, these might be valid sometimes. The question is, how often do you need to rationalize his behavior?

The perfect man does not exist. But there are plenty of men out there whose actions are fully compatible with the words they are using. Your gut feeling would not be alarmed with those men since they are consistent and authentic.

If your gut feeling tells you something is wrong, monitor his actions for a while. They won't lie.

Trap Fifteen: Jealousy

This is a trap many women have fallen victim to. We've all seen how playing hard to get works better than being easy to get when it comes to creating and keeping the attraction alive. It seems obvious, but a guy will fight more to keep his woman when he risks losing her. A guy who's interested in a woman but not yet dating her would increase his efforts when he sees that woman, his prey, flirt with another man. Right?

Some women have it all figured out and deploy the following strategy: they start to openly flirt with other men in order to make the guy they want jealous. A lot of women use this to attract a guy, and some use it to keep a guy or make him more attracted to them.

This strategy always fails.

It can have a short-term positive effect on guys whose egos will be triggered. If they were interested in the first place, they will increase their efforts. And then when they get you, they lose interest yet again. Great guys, however, will respond very negatively to the jealousy trap.

Let's first look at using jealousy to attract a guy you want to date. In this strategy, a woman will openly flirt with man A. She then hopes this will attract the other guy, guy B. A good guy will not fall for this, and even if he was attracted, he will disengage right away.

Men love to fight for a woman, chase her, and work hard to get her. Men also love competition -- look at how many men are competing in sports. Good men, however, will never want to compete in the game of love. It's an immediate disconnect.

A masculine man will never want a woman who clearly does not want him. If he sees her flirting with other men, this can only mean two things: she will flirt with anyone and is low value, or she's more interested in that other guy. She has clearly made up her mind; otherwise, she would not openly flirt with the other guy. This is a risk a good, high-value woman would never take since she knows she might be perceived as low value or create a disconnect. To a good man, a woman who is flirting with another man can only mean she wants the other guy more.

Women also use this strategy to make their current boyfriend or husband fall in love with them more. This is often their way to introduce playing hard to get into an already existing relationship.

This too will fail. At first, the man's ego will kick in and will have him act jealous or fight harder. Soon, however, the disconnect will take place. He will realize he's been played and manipulated. This strategy fails because it will make the man resent his woman.

A good guy will never accept this type of disrespectful behavior from his woman, however good her intentions were.

Jealousy is also a trap whenever you're the one who's jealous. If man has not been honest with you in the past, you'll have a very sensitive jealousy radar. This is not your fault. Still, it's not something he should "pay" for. A trick you can use to verify whether you have the right to be jealous or not is to imagine a stranger on a plane. This woman begins to tell you a story about her boyfriend who happens to have done the exact same thing your boyfriend or husband did. How would you respond? Does she have the right to be jealous? Or will you advise her to not worry? Then simply apply this advice to yourself.

Please think of the marshmallow chapter from earlier in this book. Just because you feel an urge or a certain emotion does not mean you should follow it. You can still take control and decide that it's not worth getting all worked up.

This is important to remember since jealousy will never get you the result you want. Let's look at two common possibilities:

1. His behavior is disrespectful. He's getting too close to another woman, and you have something to worry about. The question here is: will being jealous make it any better? In the short term, it may. He will quickly learn his lesson and hide it better! His behavior will seemingly change, and everything will look better on the outside. However, as I always say, a monkey wearing a suit is still a monkey. He might look different on the outside, but once he crosses the line with another woman, there's no turning back. He will continue to do it again. Jealousy is not the solution here. Finding yourself a guy who will treat you better is! The marshmallow study applies here yet again. Go for the short-term pain of breaking up in order to find long-term pleasure down the road in the arms of a guy who doesn't make you jealous.

2. Nothing's going on. The negative voice inside your head is just making you worry. This is trickier than the first situation. You're seeing ghosts and will

need to manage your own emotions and thoughts better. If you are jealous, he will try to assure you everything is fine because it is. Nevertheless, this is not the solution. Your jealousy radar will still be on high alert, and the slightest blip on the radar will make you worry again. He will reassure you a couple of times but then, unavoidably, the resentment will start to build. This is one of the best ways to suffocate your man and scare him away. If you're often in this situation, you'll have to learn to deal with the jealousy demon on your own, without his help. One of the best ways to tackle this negative voice is to get some perspective and look at his actions. If he is a good man, his actions will prove that everything is fine, and that he hasn't crossed any lines. Worrying about it or following these negative thoughts will only push him away and give you a self-fulfilling prophecy that you can avoid.

Trap Sixteen: The Ex

Every decent guy will have exes. How many exes will depend on his personality, the way he treats women, and more. In the (long) list of exes, there will always be women who are more special to him than others.

Many women fall into the trap of being jealous. "The ex" is one of his exes -- often the most recent one -- he still talks to, sees, or talks about. When you're just starting the relationship, you're right to believe she has an advantage over you. She might still be special to him. It's not that she's prettier or has a better personality per se; it's that they have a history together.

The more experiences you've shared with another person, the stronger the bond gets. They've got memories, stories, vacations, moments (good and bad) that they've shared; those experiences typically create a very strong bond.

When you begin dating a guy, he will have or have had that bond with at least one of his exes. That's OK! There is nothing you can do to take that bond away, to move ahead quicker. You can only make the bond he has with you worse! Time has to pass. You'll start building your own bond with him by going out on dates and creating those shared experiences. You cannot decrease the bond between him and his ex by badmouthing her, by asking him not to talk to her, by becoming jealous, and so on. This will only hurt you and your chances of getting ahead with him.

Many women believe they are in an invisible fight with the ex. They think they have to prove themselves. The downside is that they will be devaluating themselves. **Trying to prove you're better than the ex**

communicates that you are seeking his approval, that you believe she is better than you, that you're not feeling confident because of her, etc. It most definitely will lower your value in his eyes. Never try to qualify yourself to him for any reason, certainly not because of his ex(es).

I've explained how to use emotional intelligence earlier on in this book, and this is one of the examples where you'll need to use it. If the ex is still in the picture, you will feel bad about it. That's understandable. She has something with him that you don't have yet -- time spent together. It cannot be avoided. How you decide to handle the situation is an important choice.

Think of it this way. If he and his ex were such a good match, she wouldn't be the ex. She would still be in his life. Don't make her more important than she is by putting attention on her.

If he's still too involved with her, walk away. Reduce his value by making other aspects of your life much more important than him, or walk away altogether. Don't be jealous or cry about it. Move on. He should know how disrespectful this is to you. If you take a step back and he doesn't come after you with an apology, then it was the right call to move on and walk away. He *was* indeed still too involved with the ex, and there was no room for you. This might happen, especially if the break-up was recent and she broke up with him.

However, the trap involves guys who are over the ex. They may or may not still see the ex, but they're really over her. That's where it's important to not let the ex get to you. You are you, and the only advantage she has -- all the time she has spent with him and the bond they had -- is something that will no longer grow. You will be automatically be catching her, and time will make her memory and importance fade as you win ground and gain importance. This happens automatically, so please don't put any emphasis on the process. Focus on creating a bond with your man instead of fixating on his old bonds from past relationships.

Trap Seventeen: Your Looks

This is a tricky trap, I admit. Most men think looks are important when it comes to the woman they choose to approach. And almost every woman has felt how powerful her looks and her body can be when it comes to attracting men. It can attract some men like moths to a flame.

Don't be fooled. As I pointed out earlier, men know the importance of looks will quickly fade away once they are in a relationship with a woman.

I still remember one of my female colleagues from my old ad agency. She was pretty, seemed intelligent, and had been single for a while. I could see in her eyes that she liked me the moment she was introduced to me on her first day. It was *that* obvious. Now since I had decided to keep work and pleasure separate, I didn't flirt back, even when she started to increase her hints.

That's when she decided to crank it up a notch and add her looks to the game. I was standing at a colleague's desk in the graphical department when she had to explain something to another graphical designer. She stood across from me, with her back facing me while she bent over to point something out on the graphic designer's screen. She used a very seductive pose that immediately alerted my "hot woman in sight" radar. So I looked over. She then turned her head to me, looked at me seductively, and smiled.

She probably thought this would be a great move. And in a sense, it seemed to work; it increased my physical attraction to her. Most men, however, are not just mammals; they have more than their primal instincts. My physical attraction rose, but my opinion of her plummeted.

She seemed to be an intelligent and smart woman, so why did she think she had to behave like this to 'get' me? A few weeks later, she asked me out on a date. I politely declined.

Something interesting had happened here; it has happened more than once to me, to my friends, and to the men I often interview prior to writing a book on relationships. The trap these women step into is not that they use their looks, it is using their looks too soon.

Imagine that you're out on a first date with a great guy. When you had first met him, he seemed great. That first date, however, was different. As you sit down at the table, he orders the most expensive champagne the restaurant has to offer. Since you met him at the restaurant, you have no idea what car he drives. He, however, ostentatiously puts the keys of his Porsche in front of you on the table. You decide not to mention the brand of his car. He steps up his game and talks about what a great car he has, how it's one of the more expensive versions since he has the best option pack, and more.

As the evening progresses you can't help but wonder what he has to hide. Why does he think it's necessary to flaunt his stuff in order to get you? Is his personality not enough? What's wrong with him? You can't help it, and you start to lower his value. You're less and less interested in him as the night goes on.

A woman who uses her looks to seduce a man tries to play the same game. She will be able to attract dumb men, players, one-night-stand guys, and every other type of predator. Great guys, however, will see right through it and will lower the value they accord to her.

There is a time and place for using your looks. When you're already in a relationship or dating a guy, great men love to see you seduce them with your looks. They love it when you tease them.

Use it to seduce him while he's still brushing his teeth before coming to bed. Dance for him in a sensual way, and let him have you as a gift for being respectful, affectionate, and good to you whenever you deserved it.

Never, ever use your looks to get something from him. There will be an immediate disconnect, and your value will drop to a very low level when he senses you're using it to get something from him.

Is this a mistake you've ever made in the past? A lot of women have. It's a mistake that's easily made. Using looks to seduce him before the relationship has started or to fix the relationship later on (thus still trying to get something from him: his commitment, his love, his attention) will always backfire.

Use it as a gift to reward him for good behavior. It is one of the many powers you have as a woman. It should always be used in moderation.

Trap Eighteen: The Overlapping Circles

Imagine there are two circles. Your life is one circle, his life is yet another circle.

For some women, their relationship can only be a success when both circles totally overlap. Their life must become intertwined with the life of their guy.

I've been studying successful relationships for over 10 years; I've personally interviewed and coached hundreds of women and couples, and I've seen one common denominator in the successful couples. Their circles never totally overlap.

Even though some couples seem to get away with overlapping circles, most see their relationship deteriorate. The explanation is pretty easy. There are no passionate experiences to discuss since everything is shared. It can be suffocating to spend all of your free time together, and it eventually starts to get boring. It will start to itch first, then the frustration will rise, as if you're a wild animal trapped in a cage.

Couples who have part of their circle separate, who still have their own life have stories to tell and experiences to share ("Hey Hon, you won't believe what my friends and I did when..."). This will also create the necessary space that will make sure you won't trigger his fear of commitment.

I remember interviewing a woman who had been married to a successful and all-round great guy for 21 years. They had two teenage daughters and seemed to have a successful marriage. I'll call her Anna. One day as we were finishing up a meeting and were alone in the meeting room, I asked her for her secret.

"Well Brian, it's simple," she said. *"We make sure we still have our own, separate lives. Last weekend I went away for the entire weekend with four of my best girlfriends. We visited London and had an amazing time. My husband stayed home to look after the kids. And next month he'll do something with his buddies the entire weekend and then I'll stay home. We have the best of both worlds. We love and support each other, we have two great kids, we share the housekeeping responsibilities, we work as a team, and yet we still get many of the benefits of the single life. I get to go away with my girlfriends every now and then and feel like I have no responsibilities whatsoever. Even though I'm 43, I still get to feel like a teenager and have fun. I truly can because I know he's holding the fort while I'm gone.*

I, on the other hand, offer him the same freedom. That's what a true team is about. We both have a better life since we're together, than we could ever have being single. The best of both worlds, while we at the same time try to reduce the negatives to an absolute minimum."

This is a recurring story and strategy I saw with most happy, long-term couples I interviewed or studied.

Some women try to become one with their man. Although this can feel great in the short term, it most often doesn't work in the long term. It is crucial you never totally merge with your partner. This is the fast lane to a boring and predictable relationship where that new spark you got when you just met will quickly fade and never return.

You'll have something to talk about whenever you spend time apart and have separate experiences; you'll have exciting stories to share. My current long-term girlfriend is a psychologist who decided to do some volunteer work in Guatemala for a couple of months. When she had time for a holiday, we decided to meet up in Miami. I hadn't seen her for two months besides our Skype video calls. I still remember the feeling I had when she walked through those automated doors right after customs. I saw her and had that initial spark again. Her eyes lit up as she saw me. We fell in love with each other all over again (after we'd already been in a serious relationship for two years). This can simply not happen when you totally merge with someone. It's an often overlooked and yet important part of any long-term relationship.

Boredom and habits quickly start when you've been together for over a year. Every day, every week starts to look like the week before. Love can deal with that. Attraction cannot.

An exciting relationship is always one where love and attraction are combined. Having hobbies and activities outside of the relationship can and will help keep that spark alive in the long run.

Needless to say, what you do together counts as well. Where both circles overlap, where your life and his life merge, is important as well. This is where you'll have experiences you wouldn't possibly have without each other.

This cross-section is crucial and even overlooked by couples spending a lot of time together. This is the part where he will make your life better and where you will enhance his. A man will never leave you when his life is better with you than without you. The cross-section between both circles is where that takes place.

How can you make this cross-section exciting? Create experiences together you wouldn't have alone; share moments you would never have had if you weren't a couple. Think about going for a picnic in the park, visiting a museum, having an early morning walk on the beach, visiting any of the beautiful wonders of nature where you can watch the wildlife and enjoy the scenery. Be together and enjoy each other's company, but remember to keep it exciting! The goal is to enhance both your and his life so both you and him can realize: "I would have never had this positive experience without him/her". That's the glue in long-term relationships. That's the best reason to always stay together.

Trap Nineteen: Underestimating His Friends' Impact

Men and the way they feel about their friends has been a mystery to a lot of women. When men are friends, real friends, they don't fight or play games; they're really supporting each other and behave like a brotherhood.

It's important to men to still spend time with other men. This guy time is so significant that when a man gets deprived of this, his behavior will slowly start to change.

Typically, men understand that having a significant other means less time is available for watching football with their friends, going out, playing golf, etc. What men fear, however, is completely losing that hang-out time or receiving calls and texts asking "When will you be coming home?" when they do actually get to go out.

I've talked about the circles of life already, but just to reiterate. We all need a part of our lives where our partner is not included. For men, part of these extra relationship activities must include guy time. Some women have a hard time accepting this and may feel the need to compete with his male friends. Some women step into the "me versus them" trap, and this is a painful one with a lot of side effects.

This is a two-way street. His male friends can see his girlfriend, you, as a danger as well. I've seen it happen often; one of my friends falls in love and disappears for a couple of weeks or months. Some men never resurfaced and hang out with their wives and 2.4 kids every night of the week. While some family men may prefer this quality time with their children and spouse, most men still want to see their friends every now and then. This is healthy behavior.

Guy time is important to men. When they can take advantage of time with their friends, it will make them better men toward their girlfriends and wives. It charges their masculinity batteries, so to speak. These batteries should never be depleted. When they do get empty, men will do whatever it takes to recharge them, including lying, to spend time with men and engaging in manly activities.

Men need to feel manly. Your guy can feel and recharge his masculinity when he is protecting you, fixing something for you, taking care of you, and more. Nevertheless, part of this charge will always need to come from spending time with other men.

Does that sound ridiculous? I hope not. It's the truth.

Let's take a look at an example from one of my clients.

Carrie was dating Brendon, a guy with only a couple of true friends with whom he hung out a lot when he was single. Nothing wild, they just went to a football game, rode mountain bikes, played golf, or hung out at a bar to talk and "mastermind," as he called it.

As soon as Carrie started to date Brendon, she saw his friends as enemies. She couldn't help thinking they where stealing him away whenever he met them for guy time. Brendon was a successful dentist who didn't have too much free time, so she wanted his precious recesses in schedule to be spent with her.

As a result, Brendon's friends started to see Carrie as a threat. In their eyes, she was the girl who was trying to manipulate Brendon, forcing him to give up what once seemed important to him. They were supportive at first, but after a couple of weeks of dating, they couldn't help it and started to warn Brendon. They wanted Brendon to come to his senses and realize he was giving up on his hobbies and friends, aspects of his life that were always important to him.

This soon created a very negative and vicious cycle with two camps fighting each other while Brendon was stuck in the middle. He tried to defend Carrie whenever his friends called him out on his behavior, and at home, he tried to explain to Carrie why it was important to still see his friends. In other words, Brendon wasn't having any fun.

This is a nice example of how Carrie was decreasing the quality of his life instead of enhancing it. Carrie eventually lost the battle when Brendon broke up with her, stating that he needed some space and was unhappy with how everything had unfolded.

Carrie made a big mistake here. Most women will not be as strict as Carrie, but many will still have a hard time with guy time, especially when they're excluded from these activities.

This is a big trap since it will always launch a negative vicious cycle, especially when it's the woman who tries to forbid him from seeing his friends too often. Nevertheless bad things will happen even when it's the man who prefers spending time with his girlfriend or wife above spending time with his friends.

There's a natural reason behind this process. It's in the nature of men to spend time with other men and do manly stuff. If he feels like that will not be possible, especially when a woman gives him that feeling early on in the relationship, he will start to run in the other direction. It's important to allow guy time and if needed, push him to have guy time.

Here is why:

1. When his friends see that you support guy time, they will continuously let him know what a catch you are. They will respect you. This is obviously important if you're looking to build a long-term relationship with this man.
2. It will make you look like a high-value woman, the opposite of a needy woman.
3. It will make him long for you. When he's doing his guy stuff, that particular barrel will be filling up thus creating a void in the "spend time with my woman" barrel. When he feels this void, he will want to spend time with you and be intrinsically motivated to do so. You won't have to ask it. If this does not happen, then you can take this as a major red flag. The golden rule always applies: if you're the best version of you in the relationship and the guy doesn't behave or respond in the way you'd love him to, he's not the right guy for you.
4. He, your guy, will not feel as if he has to fight for his important guy time.
5. When something is taken away, we want it more, often more than we need it. When a woman supports her man and wants him to have guy time, he will need less of it. When she prohibits him from spending that much time with his friends, it will become all the more important to him.
6. There will be another reason for him to not have the dreadful fear of commitment.

Relationships are always a long-term game. Women who try to keep their man to themselves, who see guy-time as the enemy, are fighting a losing battle. However, women who not only allow his guy time but actually force him to have it will always win in the short and long term.

When his life is better with you than without you, he will never leave. This means you'll sometimes have to use your emotional intelligence and fight your own instincts. Your longing for instant gratification might make it hard when he wants to spend time away from you.

Here are a couple of scenarios you could find yourself in:

Your guy is invited by a good male friend to go out for dinner and drinks this Friday night. It's a friend he used to hang out with often before the two of you met. Friday is the night you like to stay in, watch a movie together, and spend some quality time. He enjoys that too so he says: "I'm going to decline the invitation. I want to stay with you." This is when your female instincts might say, "Great! Look at what a great guy I have. Sure, honey, stay here and let's watch a movie like we've done the past couple of weeks."

This is a big mistake, a trap. Can you see why?

He needs his guy time, even when he's not consciously aware of it. So if I can presuppose you're with a great guy who won't go out so he can just be with other women, you'll need to push him into going out. Even though you prefer to spend time with him, he'll need this guy time. In this example, he has been spending the last couple of weeks with you non-stop, and only spent time away from you for work-related activities. So you'll know he needs to recharge his masculinity batteries.

"Honey, I think you should go," you decide to say. He's a good guy so he responds, "No, I don't want to leave you alone. If I go I'll ask my friend if I can bring you with me."

"No, honey. Please go> I'll be fine, I've been meaning to [fill in activity that proves that you have a life of your own, not including him] and I think you'll have fun too!"

This strengthens the relationship more than you realize. It takes away fear of commitment; it recharges his batteries, and it makes him think, "Boy am I lucky to have her! My other friends can never go out alone." It makes his friends see you as a respectful and loving girlfriend/wife.

You'll see change in his behavior the morning after his "man date". He will be more affectionate and caring. He'll feel like a man. His masculinity battery will have been recharged.

Have you ever used this strategy where he too wanted to stay with you, but you fought your own instincts and told him to have fun? Please give it a try. You'll be surprised of the results.

A closely related scenario is the one where you are out with him and his friends; it's still early and you, for some reason, would prefer to go home. He's still having fun since the night is still young. What do you do?

Some women will ask him to leave now and go home together. If he asks to stay a little longer, they may turn on the nagging engine and increase the pressure. If he's a bad guy, he will be unaffected by it and continue to have fun. If he's a good guy, he will be affected and decide to leave with her. She will then feel good (instant gratification); he, on the other hand, will start to feel some form of resentment. The same feeling a kid feels when you take his lollipop away.

As will often be the case, a good guy will give in to your request and take you home. No second requests required. He won't feel resentment in this optional scenario, but if this happens a lot, he'll feel he's missing out on a lot of positive feelings because of his girlfriend, the one who always wants to go home when he's still having fun.

The best possible outcome in this scenario, with the most positive long-term effects on the relationship, is saying, "Honey, I'm tired and want to leave, but I want you to stay here and have fun. I'll take a cab or Sandra will drive me home." Any bad guy will then reply, "OK. See you later, alligator" as he dances away into the night. A good guy will say, "No, honey. I'll come with you" or at least "OK. Let me call you a cab and wait with you outside." The goal here is to let him continue to have fun. You're going to bed anyway.

As you are returning home alone, three things will happen in his mind.

1. He'll think, "Wow, what a great girlfriend I have! She's so supportive and cool." He will continue to have fun for a while, then start to miss you too much and return home.
2. He will not have had the lollipop effect or link you to any negative feelings to what happened that night.

That's another example of how you can use spending time away from each other as glue that significantly strengthens the bond between you and him.

Trap Twenty: The Contract, Part I

Here's a standard scenario many couples experience. You stay over at his place, and he does something you're not pleased with. He leaves the toilet seat up, or he doesn't throw his dirty underwear in the laundry bin. Most women will decide it's wise to not say anything about these unpleasant habits of his. It seems like a wise choice because you don't want to come across as someone who nags.

It's also not *that* big of a deal. He's not your full-time roommate, after all. You're only forced to endure his sloppiness when you stay over at his place and maybe when he stays over at yours. Here's a first important warning though: take notes if you see any of his bad habits while he's staying over at your place. He's supposed to be showing you his best behavior.

When the couple moves in together, most women find out his bad habits are indeed, habits. He just keeps repeating them without thinking. Some women start to mention them in an effort to "fix" the problem. Your man may get flustered and reply, "But baby, you never made a big deal of it before. Why are you starting to complain about it now? I don't get it!"

This can lead to friction or fights. Frustration and resentment starts to build up between both parties and before you know it, staying together just isn't fun anymore.

When you buy a puppy, you need to train it right away. You can't let it sleep on the bed, only to change that rule later. Puppies don't understand when you change the rules. Men don't either.

When something bothers you, the right time to bring it up is immediately. If you wait too long, it might be too late to change it. It's important to talk about the habits that annoy you before you move in together. It will only get worse when you share the same apartment or house. Sure, you need to pick your battles. You can't mold him into the perfect guy.

The best strategy is to decide what the real deal breakers are. When something he does or says bothers you, ask yourself: "If I move in with this guy, and we live together for the rest of my days, could I live with him doing/saying this?" If the answer is no, you have a second choice to make. Ask yourself, "Am I overreacting? If a good friend of mine would tell me her boyfriend does/says this, what would I tell her? Would I say it's a deal breaker to her too?" If the answer is no to either of these questions, you'll need to decide to pick your battles and not mention it to him.

If, on the other hand, the answer is yes, you need to tell him now. It's a risk worth taking. After all, if you don't do it now, you'll have to do it when you've moved in together and you'll both be so much more invested (both financially, emotionally, and time wise) than you are now.

When you start to date, both of you are creating an unwritten contract of what is OK and what is not. You'll need to guard your side of the contract and make sure it states your deal breakers. When you mention them, you should choose a non-nagging form of communication. Assertively say, "Hon, I really don't like it when you _____" or "Hon, it makes me feel bad/unhappy/ when you _____." If you're with a great guy, this should at the very least open up the conversation about this topic, so he can share his point of view as well.

If he's still not changing his behavior, you can enforce the rule a bit more by using positive psychology. For instance, you can say, "I love a guy who [insert whatever he is not doing]." If he still doesn't change, you'll need to anticipate he never will.

Trap Twenty One: The Contract, Part II

Fairy tales allow us to believe that love is unconditional and lasts forever. Love will also conquer everything and cannot be broken. This, sadly, is far from the truth, as reality proves every single day. Just look at the divorce rate. Most of those people truly meant it when they said, "For better and for worse."

If "worse" lasts too long, love won't be enough.

The minute you start dating the two of you start creating an unwritten contract. When a man decides to walk over to initiate the flirtation process, he has decided that you've just passed the physical attraction test. He likes the way you look. You, in turn, will have to decide whether his looks cut it or not. If he's sufficiently attractive, his looks get written in the contract as well.

This is a crucial first part that some people overlook. The "looks" department of the contract will remain somewhat important. Just imagine you've met a great looking guy; it's clear he takes care of his body, and you like that. After two months of dating, however, he feels like he has you and can decrease his "get a woman attracted to me by taking care of my body" efforts. As a result, he stops working out and decides to spend his nights on the couch while hydrating himself with beer. Not long after, his waist size starts to expand significantly. Two months later, his good-looking body is nowhere to be found, and you need a bigger couch.

Does this mean your level of attraction to him can now change? It sure does! He has changed part of the contract, part of what made you attracted to him in the first place. This, of course, goes both ways.

We're not *that* superficial; the looks department is merely the first bullet point of the contract. Soon after the dating phase started, other bullet points were added that become way more important than physical attraction, as I mentioned earlier on in this book. Those points were created when you had conversations about ambitions, values, hobbies, and so on. These are all part of both of your personalities, and they will become a very important part of the contract. After the contract is crafted, you both decide whether or not to continue spending time together based on personality, values, and so on.

Most people don't even realize this contract exists, but it always does. The moment one of or even both parties start to deviate from the unwritten contract, frustration will rise and the first fights will start to emerge.

When you have a fight with a guy, it's because he did something unexpected and incompatible with the contract, you had a disconnect. You may find yourself saying, "When we started dating, you would have never talked to me in this disrespectful way" or "When we were first dating, you always showed up on time."

This contract is important and can serve you in two ways. First, make sure that you remain true to who you were in the early stages of the relationship. That's what made him fall madly in love with you. When you deviate from that, consider it striking through the bullet points of the contract. If you continue to do this, there will come a point where he may decide he just doesn't feel it anymore. Second, make sure you add bullet points to the contract too. As I've already mentioned, high-value women love to assert their needs and wants. Men, being the chasers, will often try to live up to them. Here are some bullet points you should always add :

- "Hon, I don't like it when you _____ because it hurts me."
- "Hon, it's important to me that you _____."

You can go back to the deal-breaker questions I mentioned in the previous trap. Whenever a guy performs one of those deal breakers, you need to speak up. Right away. Create a new bullet point, or refer to ones already in your unwritten contract.

Some women wait too long to speak up and then get a reaction like, "Why are you so needy/high-maintenance/difficult? You never said anything about this when we first started dating. This is just who I am..." If that's how he's going to react, you obviously deserve better. Any man who isn't willing to listen to your concerns is not the right guy for you. You are better off finding this out sooner than later, so don't be afraid to speak up.

Conclusion

You've made it! And I want to congratulate you.

Some of these traps are obvious and yet I keep meeting women who forget to apply them. It's a mistake we all make in many areas of our lives. There so much we 'know' or that sounds obvious when we hear it and yet we fail to apply it in our lives.

I hope this book has installed some alarm bells that will start to ring as soon as you come near any of the traps I've mentioned. That's the best way to avoid them.

Relationships are hard, even with the right guy. Don't be fooled by all of those seemingly perfectly happy couples you see posting pictures on social media. Even though they might be happy, the road to their happiness was long and never ends; even they have ups and downs. The 'they lived happily ever after' does not exist. Every relationship requires hard work at all times. Men and women are not alike, physically nor emotionally. On top of that we all have different personalities, wants and desires. These are all obstacles that need to be overcome, day in and day out.

And that's fine! That's the way life is supposed to be.

One of the major 'life traps' I see some of my clients fall into is that they are looking for the perfect job, the perfect relationship, the perfect everything. They're trying to find that moment of total happiness where there isn't a worry, disruption or problem in sight. That moment does not exist. Everyone always has some obstacle to deal with. The obstacle is the way.

Relationships will always be filled with challenges. That's a given, and that's also the reason why it is so important to make sure you find the right guy to start with. Being in a relationship with the perfect guy for you will be hard enough.

I cannot stress this enough: Filter out all of the bad guys fast. Don't wait for your relationship to get better or for your man to get his act together. If he's not behaving like the guy you want and you can honestly say your expectations are realistic and normal, start dating again and find another guy. A relationship is hard enough even with the perfect guy for you. So you absolutely need to weed out the bad ones.

Two of my other books can come in handy here.

Red Flags: how to know he's playing games with you

This is an important book because it will explain how to avoid the men that will hurt you, the men that are only out to use you, manipulate you, and play games with your heart. Then, once you have the right guy on the hook, it's important not to lose him.

My book *Are You Scaring Him Away* deals with that subject in depth.

Overall, I want you to remember one thing: *Never adapt or change to keep a guy.* We only live once, and life is too short to try to please other people who wouldn't want us to stay when we show our true persona.

We all deserve someone who loves us for who we are. As I explained in the first chapter of this book, self-control and emotional intelligence can be your biggest allies throughout your life. They allow you to be the best version of yourself.

Finding a guy you can be happy with is quite a daunting task. You might want to say, "I give up! I'll just stay with *this* guy even though he _____." Please don't do this. Finding the right guy is like winning the lottery. You can only win the lottery by playing a lot. In this case, you can only find the right man by meeting a ton of guys and filtering out the bad ones. That's the power you have as a woman. When you correctly position yourself in the presence of men, the right guys will start to move in.

Here are two important remarks to remember:

1. Fish in the right pool. What guy do you want to be with? Where would that guy hang out? What kind of hobbies might he have? What kind of social gatherings does he attend? In other words, where can you go so the right one can see you and introduce himself to you? A lot of younger women go out to bars and clubs to meet guys. That's fine, if you're looking for a guy who likes to hang out in bars and clubs a lot. If I want to see a wild Zebra, I need to go to his natural habitat where he always hangs out. Where does your type of guy hang out? Go to his natural habitat. That's where you have the highest possibility of meeting him right away, without having to weed out a ton of bad guys.

2. Remember the trap where I talked about going against the grain and not following nature's way? You'll need to position yourself in his habitat somewhere. He, however, needs to move in and take the lead. You'll save yourself a lot of time and heartbreak when you let him do the chasing. That's

your best and first filter. Men who don't put in the effort will be trouble down the road.

I can say I've waited for more than ten years for the girl I'm currently dating. She was well worth the wait. Like you, I've had to weed out the bad ones and decide I wouldn't settle for less than I deserved (realistically). To this day, I'm glad I did. There were so many instant-gratification opportunities that I consciously had to walk away from, but it was all worth it in the end.

I hope you've enjoyed reading this book. I've loved writing it for you. Picturing you reading my words, getting some AHA moments, applying it in your life, and getting better results with men inspire me to keep writing. I hope my book will serve you well.

Good luck!
Brian

PS. **And if you want even more tips and strategies**, sign up for my FREE advanced tactics newsletter on ScaringHimAway.com and join the 64,437 women who already receive it.

Other Works by the Author

*F*CK Him! - Nice Girls Always Finish Single - "A guide for sassy women who want to get back in control of their love life"*

Red Flags: how to know he's playing games with you

Are You Scaring Him Away

Failure to launch: How to handle your Commitment-phobic Man

Made in the USA
Las Vegas, NV
05 February 2024

85351426R00075